Following Alice

A LIFE IN TEACHING

by Anne Ayers Koch

*To Roberto
with every in
good wish in
your vocation
Anne Ayers Koch*

LUMINARE PRESS

EUGENE, OREGON

Following Alice: A Life in Teaching
© 2013 Anne Ayers Koch

Printed in the United States of America

Cover illustration: Cathy Kapelka; design: Claire Flint

Luminare Press
467 W 17th Ave
Eugene, OR 97401
www.luminarepress.com

LCCN: 2013941920

ISBN: 978-1-937303-15-0

FINDING ALICE

BY ANNE AYERS KOCH

The first wonder is the offspring of ignorance;
the last is the parent of adoration.
—Samuel Taylor Coleridge

In memory of

VICTOR ANDREW NIGRO

October 20, 1969 – September 15, 1987

Oh! I have slipped the surly bonds of Earth
And danced the skies on laughter-silvered wings;
And, while with silent, lifting mind I've trod
The high untrespassed sanctity of space,
Put out my hand, and touched the face of God."
—"High Flight,"
John Gillespie Magee, Jr.

CONTENTS

PREFACE xiii

INTRODUCTION: On The Riverbank 1
Broad Stripes and Bright Stars
Is Someone Knocking?
The Other Side of the Moon
At the Movies

PART ONE
CONFUSED AND CONFOUNDED
DO YOU NEED IT?

CHAPTER ONE: Down The Rabbit Hole 19
What's in a Name?
Time Interrupted
Anywhere But Here

CHAPTER TWO: The Pool Of Tears 33
Lend a Hand?
From Monolith to Mosaic
Sink or Swim

CHAPTER THREE: The Caucus Race And A Long Tale 43
Fairies in the Mist
You See WHAT?
Yesterday's Model

PART TWO
CALCULATE AND CONNECT
WHAT DO YOU KNOW?

CHAPTER FOUR: The Rabbit Sends In A Little Bill 59

Growing Pains

Elephants and Gorillas

Unknown Unknowns

CHAPTER FIVE: Advice From A Caterpillar 73

Why Not?

The Radio Dial

Where to Begin?

PART THREE
CREATE
WHAT DO YOU NEED TO KNOW?

CHAPTER SIX: Pig And Pepper 89

Unexpected Destination

Who's Here?

Boxes, Banners, and Batwings

CHAPTER SEVEN: A Mad Tea Party 107

Plenty of Room

Puzzles, Parables, and Prizes

A Golden Key

Coda: A Golden Key

PART FOUR
CULTIVATE AND COACH
WHAT IS THE BEST DESIGN STRATEGY?

CHAPTER EIGHT: The Queen's Croquet Ground 127

Precision Tools

Through Different Eyes

Independent Minds

CHAPTER NINE: The Mock Turtle's Story 139

Cooking Secrets
What Else Had You to Learn?
The Twelfth Day

Part Five
CALIBRATE
DID IT WORK?

CHAPTER TEN: The Lobster Quadrille 153

Join the Dance?
Adventures First

CHAPTER ELEVEN: Who Stole The Tarts? 165

Consider the Verdict
Not Quite Finished
A Curious Sensation

Part Six
CELEBRATE
LAUGHTER AND TEARS

CHAPTER TWELVE: Alice's Evidence 183

Proper Places
Meaning After All
A Wonderful Dream

EPILOGUE 197
ACKNOWLEDGMENTS 201
ABOUT THE AUTHOR 203

It's what you learn after you know it all that counts.
—John Wooden

PREFACE

*H*ow does someone arrive at a career?

By design? Default? Duress? For me it was a toy train, a twinkling tree, and a four-year-old's imagination—the place most adventures begin.

The heavy black engine pulled a boxy coal car. Next came an orange flatbed—perfect for hauling marbles and wooden sewing spools. A boxy red caboose brought up the rear. The child imagined waving goodbye from the caboose's tiny back platform, like an old-fashioned politician, as she traveled on adventures beyond the Christmas house.

I spent hours that holiday season moving freight, taking trips, building cities around the elongated track with magazines and books. It was important work. Although there were wooden blocks in the toy chest, Dad's hardback books were much better construction material. With their heavy leather covers and gold-embossed spines, they made perfect walls, towers, and bridges. I can think of few better ways to introduce a child to books than to let her stack them, upend them, rearrange them, pretend to read them. The silvery oval, surrounded by its book buildings, led the child to a career destination—the mysterious, maligned, magical world of school.

The essays here are an affectionate recounting of that journey—a journey that began with books and ended with people. It followed a path from lessons prescribed by experts for someone else's students to curricula my students and I created together. I moved from a role as "dispenser of information" to one of teacher as co-designer and coach.

The trip is propelled by Lewis Carroll's *Alice's Adventures in Wonderland.* On one level Carroll's story is an enchanting childhood tale. On another it is an inspired journey offering a view of the modern world that has yielded almost as many quotations as the Bible, Shakespeare's plays, or the poems of Pope or Byron.

Alice's journey took her beyond her conventional Victorian childhood to a world where caterpillars talk, cats appear and disappear at will, a white rabbit wears tiny gloves, carries a magic fan, and uses a pocket watch that reminds him he is late. As she faces the unexpected, unconventional, and sometimes unpleasant characters in Wonderland, Alice grows up. Grows more willing to accept change. More willing to challenge unfairness.

My journey in schools was its own kind of Wonderland. It became a place of expanded focus. Wider vistas. Longer perspectives. Shifts. From narrow concentration on content to broader concerns about community. From a shallow view of religion as separate denominations with esoteric rules to a deeper appreciation of unanswerable questions. From needing to measure progress to understanding Einstein's observation: "The fairest thing we can experience is the mysterious. It is the fundamental emotion which stands at the cradle of true art and true science. He who knows it not, who can no longer wonder, can no longer feel amazement, is as good as dead, a snuffed-out candle."

At first, classroom management mattered most. Then content coverage. Then test scores. All of those do matter. But they're not everything. And often they don't matter most. Decades passed. In addition to celebrating student mastery of society's academic expectations I began cheering their less-heralded but equally important personal achievements—shy students who overcame fear of public speaking, bullies who became more compassionate, non-readers who found something redeeming in a book, graphic artists who had a chance to analyze in images what others conveyed in words, intellectual cynics who moved a little closer to hope.

Lewis Carroll's unsuspecting Alice, tired of sitting on the river-bank, followed the rabbit down the large hole under the hedge to the edge of the "loveliest garden you ever saw." How could she find a way into those beds of bright flowers and cool fountains? Her escapades led her to understand her world and herself better.

They were not unlike my own sense-making search. Her adventure lasted one afternoon. Mine a lifetime. Down different rabbit holes both of us learned about ourselves, the world we thought we knew, and the folks who live there. We also learned Wonderland isn't somewhere else. It's right here if we can see beyond the barriers that separate people when we insist on "us and them."

It's really only us.

Introduction

ON THE RIVERBANK

The unconscious mind wants stories. When we see two phenomena, we are quick to make up stories to link and explain them. Story making—you might call it model building—is a large part of what the mind does. We have an experiencing self and a remembering self, and the remembering self is more powerful.
—David Brooks,
The Social Animal

BROAD STRIPES AND BRIGHT STARS

*T*he heavyset girl slumped at her desk, a dark blot on the spring sun streaming through the windows. Her long stringy hair matched the dirty mop in the janitor's bucket outside the door. Excited conversations danced on dust motes riding the sunbeams as her classmates talked about the upcoming prom. What to wear? Where to eat? Where to go afterwards? She wasn't invited. To the dance. To the parties. To anything.

She watched the animated expressions around her behind a mask that said, "It doesn't matter." It did matter. I had been outside enough groups to know. That day I was the teacher—a different kind of outsider in the social norms of high school. Separate. Invisible. So was she. Outsiders see things insiders miss. Hidden by agreement. By accident. By apologists for the status quo. It was 1989. I remembered another girl.

I went to ten schools before high school graduation. Not all in the same town, same state, even the same coast. It was a Navy childhood, a childhood on the move. The schools ranged from rural North Carolina to staid New England to mercurial Washington, D.C. to progressive California. Some were in small towns. Others in urban corridors. Still others in sleepy suburbs. I attended one school twice, separated by a year-long cross-country reassignment.

Through all the changes, the myriad classrooms, the teachers—good, bad, indifferent—one thing that stayed with me is the intensity of the experience. The years before college are a rite of passage most of us share. We meet it not ready for what we find—the kindness and cruelty, the exhilaration and excruciating boredom, the sorting and shaping of our self-image and worldview.

What lies on the other side of school? For a woman college graduate, choices were limited. Nursing or teaching topped the list. Even though there were thousands of occupations in government brochures that chronicle what people do—from agronomist to yodeler—most were not available to women.

I couldn't imagine myself poking and prodding sick people for a living, despite having read Helen Wills as a young teenager. Wills wrote a series of 27 mystery novels with hospital settings. Cherry Ames was the central character. The first two books chronicled her training.

That was as far as I got, despite her cute friends with their stylish uniforms and perky starched white hats. About then I had my appendix out. Cherry Ames didn't fit my experience with nurses, stitches, and a male doctor who kept pushing his hand into my side asking, "Is that tender?" as I curled into a tiny ball around the pain.

On the other hand, I was an inquisitive, cooperative student. Curiosity and cooperation may be positive attributes, but they don't guarantee success on the other side of the desk. I never thought about what teachers did. As far as I could tell the answer was "not very much." They assigned worksheets, chapters to outline, books to report on. Sometimes they lectured. They watched us work. How hard could that be?

This goes to show that while I was then and still am a voracious reader, books will only get you so far. John Locke cautioned, "Reading furnishes the mind only with materials of knowledge; it is thinking that makes what we read ours." He didn't go far enough. It takes more than thinking. It takes doing.

Despite being clueless about the profession, my belief in schools was born of excursions back and forth across America. No matter where we lived, no matter how different the schools looked, they had one thing in common—an American flag. Schools told the story of our fragile experiment. A story that required educated citizens.

Teaching was a way to contribute—a worldview shaped by my patriotic family and punctuated by schoolday rituals across the country: raising the flag, reciting the Pledge of Allegiance, reading about pilgrims and pioneers. Reinforced by writers. Writers like Ray Bradbury, whose *Fahrenheit 451* and its world without books terrified me. It was Bradbury who said, "If you don't know how to read, you don't know how to decide. We're a democracy of readers, and we should keep it that way."

Education and democracy. Connected. Complicated. Democracy requires more than knowing how to read. Education is more than covering material. Teachers focus on course content. Parents on "enrichment" activities to bolster their children's college chances. Meanwhile, students mourn the loss of childhood. "School is preparation for life," say earnest adults. It's not encouraging. Young people see more than reading, writing, and arithmetic in their classrooms. As the Mock Turtle told Alice, "The regular course was Reeling and Writhing; and then the different branches of Arithmetic—Ambition, Distraction, Uglification, and Derision."

Lewis Carroll's Alice in Wonderland has been described as looking at the world while standing on your head. The same can be said of the decision to teach school. Seeing familiar things in unexpected ways can be a gift or a curse. Sometimes it is both at once. Whether the observer is an insider or outsider, student or teacher, schools are places by turns full of wonder and terror, magic and misery.

One thing for certain. They aren't preparation for life.

They are life.

...suddenly a White Rabbit with pink eyes ran close by her. When
the Rabbit actually took a watch out of his waistcoat-pocket, and
looked at, and then hurried on, Alice started to her feet, for it
flashed across her mind that she had never before seen a rabbit
with either a waistcoat-pocket, or a watch to take out of it, and
burning with curiosity, she ran across the field after it...
—Chapter One,
Alice's Adventures in Wonderland

IS SOMEONE KNOCKING?

*M*oney matters. When it comes to schools, people say
inadequate funding is the root of our deteriorating
system. The solution? More money. It's not that simple. If it
were, the problem would be solved by now.

Huddled with 30 other aspiring teachers on the steps of UCLA's
Royce Hall, I listened as the professor explained the plan for the
"Introduction to Teaching" field course:

"You'll spend three weeks in three different high schools, observing,
assisting, and toward the end of each rotation, teaching. Afterwards,
if you're interested you can apply to the credential program."

As an afterthought he said, "Be sure to pick up a copy of 'Tips
for Classroom Management' with your schedule."

It had been a scant four years since my own high school experience. I didn't think managing was something I needed. It didn't seem
anyone managed me or my friends. I slipped the one-page list in my
binder without a glance.

Crenshaw High School—South Los Angeles. On the gray spring
morning I arrived it took less than three minutes to realize it was different from any high school I'd seen before. Opened a year earlier, it

was a gleaming collection of shiny institutional boxes looming out of the disordered gloom of a drab, disheveled, defeated neighborhood. A tall fence surrounded the campus. An LAPD car sat in front.

Since the assassinations of Martin Luther King, Jr., and Robert Kennedy, Los Angeles had become a tense, edgy place. Schools began to require identification badges. Common enough today, then they screamed OUTSIDER or worse, STUDENT TEACHER. The harried office clerk tilted her head toward the door. "Go that way," she said.

Which way? I joined the crush of teenagers coursing down the hall like lemmings heading off a cliff. People jostled for narrow openings, elbows extended. Backpacks were battering rams or shields. Everyone was yelling. I couldn't tell if they were conversations or arguments bouncing like strobe lights off the metal lockers.

As I swept along two things struck me. First—the reason the halls were so crowded. They were lined with reams and reams of paper, overhead projectors, movie screens, and boxes with the word "SUPPLIES" scrawled across them.

The supplies were the result of the federal "War on Poverty" grants that dumped hundreds of thousands of dollars into urban schools like Crenshaw. But there was no staff to monitor their distribution, or order replacement bulbs for the projectors. And even in a new school, there was inadequate storage. There wasn't any place to put the windfall supplies. It was a depressing glimpse of another in a long series of failed initiatives that have dogged public education.

Second—staff taught behind locked doors. Most days my master teacher began with six or seven students in class. During the 50-minute period others appeared, pounding the heavy door like angry woodpeckers. The teacher snapped back and forth from the podium to the door like a yo-yo on a short string. Meanwhile, the on-time arrivals left early. It was like teaching in a bus station.

My turn to teach came. I showed the teacher the management tips from our placement packets. He scanned it, grimaced, and said, " Use it for scratch paper." Panicked, I mimicked him. My door technique was a quick side step, like a football player marking the angle of a kick before a field goal. I got the same results he did. Disinterest from some. Disgust from others. Defiance from most.

Twenty years later Rodney King, a parolee high on drugs and alcohol, was caught on videotape being beaten by four LAPD officers who pulled him over after a high-speed chase through South Central LA past Crenshaw. The rioting that followed left 55 people dead, more than 2000 injured, and large swaths of the city on fire. King, who suffered from untreated addictions and learning disabilities, later won a $3.8 million judgment against the city. Not equipped for the notoriety that followed, he died in 2012 at age 47 in his backyard pool in nearby Rialto.

We still haven't found the key to unlock the potential trapped in the spreading urban wasteland. The answer doesn't lie in school alone. Protestant-educated, Spanish-Catholic philosopher George Santayana described himself as a critical realist. He said, "A child only educated at school is an uneducated child." Crenshaw was proof in the '60s. Rodney King in the '90s.

I told myself things had to be better at the next placement. They weren't. They were different. One day in the new location convinced me money wasn't the singular problem.

The next assignment: Beverly Hills High School.

"Would you tell me, please," said Alice, a little timidly, "why are you painting those roses?"
Five and Seven said nothing, but looked at Two. Two began, in a low voice, "Why, the fact is, you see, Miss, this here ought to have been a red rose-tree, and we put a white one in by mistake; and, if the Queen was to find it out, we should all have our heads cut off, you know."
—Chapter Eight,
Alice's Adventures in Wonderland

THE OTHER SIDE OF THE MOON

*D*istance is more than miles traveled. Beverly Hills High School isn't geographically far from the inner city. It might as well be. It's a different country.

BHHS is the only public high school in Los Angeles to receive money from an on-campus oil tower. The original building is a large, imposing French Normandy structure. Hanging above the wide marble lobby was a banner with the school motto, "Today Well Lived." Its famous gymnasium was featured in the 1946 Frank Capra movie classic, *It's a Wonderful Life*. The floor retracts to reveal a 25-yard-long swimming pool underneath. James Stewart and Donna Reed jitterbugged their way into the water, followed by most of the other high school revelers in Bedford Falls en route to learning three lessons:

- No one is a failure who has friends.
- Being important is mostly a matter of point of view.
- The pursuit of money as an end in itself is the root of a great deal of evil.

Chaucer's pilgrims learned the same lessons on their trip to Canterbury. The lessons didn't stick—in the 15th century, the 20th, or, if the news is any indication, now.

In 1969 the student body was mostly white, and better dressed than their teachers by a long shot. Today they are still better dressed, but the population is 47 percent Persian-speaking, 27 percent Asian, the rest Caucasian. Despite inter-district transfer incentives, it is only 2 percent African American. Unlike the Crenshaw students, who were seldom there physically, the BHHS students were barely there mentally. They tolerated their teachers either with bemused indulgence, or as an inconvenience.

Reading Suzanne Collins' description of the ruling city of Panem in her book *The Hunger Games* years later, Beverly Hills and its high school popped unbidden into my mind:

> *The cameras haven't lied about its grandeur. If anything, they have not quite captured the magnificence of the glistening buildings in a rainbow of hues that tower into the air, the shiny cars that roll down the wide paved streets, the oddly dressed people with bizarre hair and painted faces who have never missed a meal. All the colors seem artificial, the pinks too deep, the greens too bright, the yellows painful to the eyes, like the flat round disks of hard candy we can never afford to buy at the tiny sweet shop in District 12.*

Two eleventh-grade girls sitting in back of the American literature class I was assigned to had a mini beauty-salon operation underway. One polished her fingernails and those of the girls around her every day. She lined up a rainbow of nail polish colors, emery boards, cuticle scissors, and a box of Kleenex at the start of class. Business was brisk.

The girl next to her set up a battery-operated make-up mirror. Twelve inches across, it had little light bulbs around the frame. In front rested an impressive collection of bottles, brushes, lipsticks, and mascara wands. She used them all. Finished, she passed the mirror on. It was serious work at ten o'clock in the morning.

The master teacher told me, "Just ignore it. If you confront them you risk alienating them. They're popular and everyone will follow their lead."

Might be better than feeling invisible, I thought. But I supposed the teacher knew best. I followed his advice. The lighted mirror blinked around the room like a giant firefly. The pungent smell of polish remover wafted through the air.

I knew the students learned nothing the three weeks I was there—from the regular teacher or from me. On the other hand, I learned "Dusty Rose" was a versatile nail polish color.

Two decades later, in a writing class I taught, a few students came from the girls' school across the street to our all male campus. One Friday I noticed a girl painting her nails. Scowling at her fingers splayed on the desk, she alternated two colors.

"What are you DOING?" I asked, proving, despite clichés to the contrary, there are dumb questions. What she was doing was clear. But why?

"I'm trying out these colors. They don't belong to me. I have a special date this weekend. I'm deciding which one to buy."

"Just do the left hand so you can write…and see me after class," I said.

When the bell rang she lingered, clutching the classwork in her right hand.

"I did the assignment," she said with a sheepish grin, dropping it on the desk.

"Good for you. I wanted to mention I have some experience with 'Dusty Rose.' Check it out. It goes with everything."

She gaped at me. I winked.

The Beverly Hills rotation had been good for something after all. It only took 20 years to figure out what.

Money insulates—makes it easy to buy a dozen nail polish colors. It doesn't ensure good decision-making. Or good schools.

More is sometimes just more.

The dream-child moving through a land
Of wonders wild and new,
In friendly chat with bird or beast—
And half believe it's true.
—Prologue,
Alice's Adventures in Wonderland

AT THE MOVIES

*T*here's an ancient Jewish tale of a rabbi who came to synagogue with two slips of paper, one in each of his front pockets. In one pocket the slip read, "You are nothing but dust and ashes." In the other the slip read, "The world was created for you." His point—when taken together both statements are true. Before the final student-teacher placement, I would have said it's more dust and ashes. Discouraged, I trudged up the stairs of University High School.

Located in West Los Angeles, near the Santa Monica border, most University High students came from Westwood, Brentwood, and Bel Air. Opened in 1924, it was originally named Warren G. Harding High School, after the president died in 1923, 882 days into office. One of our worst chief executives ever, his name became synonymous with incompetence, corruption, and clandestine trysts with his mistress in an Oval Office closet. After UCLA moved its campus from East Hollywood to Westwood in 1929, Harding High quietly morphed into University High.

The district allows the film industry to use the campus during school hours. The only Los Angeles high school with any pre-World War II buildings remaining, its traditional, dignified structures make it a popular choice.

Filming was underway. Once again I navigated crowded hallways. They weren't filled with school supplies but with set construction clut-

ter—stacked paint cans, plywood, and lockers on wheels being rolled
from one place to another. During my three weeks at Uni, my master
teacher moved four times. Teachers complained, but the district got
paid for allowing film crews on campus. The rate was hundreds of
dollars per day. In more recent years it was $2500. It was then and
is now still too much money to pass up. In 2006 Uni was the location for the hit movie "Akeelah and the Bee." A story based on a real
experience, the filmmaker spent ten years turning a documentary on
inner-city schools into a mainstream film. But the inner-city schools
themselves were too bleak to use. University High School became
the backdrop. Change is easy in the movies.

Uni students were fun. Relaxed. Dressed in colorful "beach
clothes," they were interested in school. As I staggered through my
demonstration expository writing lessons, they were sympathetic.
They tried to follow the jerky, formulaic lesson plan I stuck to no
matter what. Occasionally one or another would stop after class and
say, "Why don't you try this…tomorrow?" Comfortable with student
teachers, most appeared to have a proprietary interest in our success.
It was sweet and surprising. For the first time I wondered who is the
student and who is the teacher in schools?

The high school has a long-famous roster of alums. Among their
graduates are Judy Garland, Elizabeth Taylor, and Marilyn Monroe.
On the other hand, they also have H.R. Haldeman, infamous from
the Nixon years, and Lynnette "Squeaky" Fromme, who tried to
assassinate Gerald Ford.

It was my most successful placement. At least the students came
to class and did the assignments. "Successful" wasn't quite the right
word…but it was a start.

Knowing I didn't have money for graduate school, the professor
wrote on my final evaluation, "Try Catholic schools—they don't require
credentials." Today that sounds insulting. Then, it was a lifeline.

The Archdiocese of Los Angeles covers three counties and 8762 square miles. From the 21 original missions stringing from San Diego to San Francisco, the church grew to 288 parishes. I sent resumes to every one with a school. The motto of the Archdiocese is, "We commit ourselves to be a community of faith and love." That commitment didn't extend to acknowledging they received my letters. I called them. Some hung up on me. Some left me on hold until I heard the dial tone. All but three turned down my request for an informational interview after I answered their first question: "Are you Catholic?"

With graduation two weeks away I resigned myself to retail work, my college summer job. The LA smog and beach fog wrapping the campus in a brown-gray shroud matched my mood. Four years of college. No job prospects. No money. Now what?

The telephone rang. A cheerful voice pierced the gloom.

"This is Sister Jeanne Heinisch. I'm the English Department Chair at Saint Monica's High school in Santa Monica. I'm looking for Anne Ayers."

"Speaking."

"I have a question," she said.

"No, I'm not Catholic."

"That wasn't my question. Can you manage a student newspaper? We're having trouble keeping an advisor."

"I worked on my high school paper. I know what it takes to get one out."

"Come see me. Let's talk."

Five words were all it took to begin a lifetime love affair with Catholic schools. An affair punctuated, as they always are, with wild swings from joy to despair. It's like Robert Frost's "lover's quarrel with the world." The poem is one of his most difficult to understand. The last line is the clearest. We all have quarrels with the world. Catholic schools were one of mine. Hard to understand. Hard to change. Impossible not to care about.

With hopes high, a $6000 salary, a student roster of 175 teenagers in five classes, the school newspaper, and the key to my own classroom, I crossed off each summer day. Back-to-school ads began to appear in the bulky *Los Angeles Times*. The nuns held a brief orientation. "No pants. No sandals. No jewelry."

I knew the first verse to Chuck Berry's "School Days" and would burst into song at odd moments.

Up in the mornin' and out to school
The teacher is teachin' the Golden Rule
American history and practical math
You studyin' hard and hopin' to pass...

I was ready.

September arrived at last, like a long-anticipated meeting with an old friend. School days…again. This time I wouldn't be a student. The teacher! I spent the final summer week practicing facial expressions in my tiny bathroom mirror. Eyebrows up. Eyebrows down. Delight. Disapproval. Dismay. Interest. Irritation. Curiosity. Concern.

Ready. No question.

St. Monica's wasn't an inner-city school or a wealthy school, or a famous school. It was a middle-class school. I was a middle-class person. I had my "Tips for Classroom Management," read all the books in the 10th-grade curriculum, and worked on my own high school paper, so what could possibly go wrong?

I soon learned. Almost everything.

Part One

Confused And Confounded

Do You Need It?

There is only one justification for instruction. It is that one or more people cannot yet do something and there is a need for them to be able to do it.
—Robert F. Mager,

CHAPTER ONE

DOWN THE RABBIT HOLE

The images of God are many. The unpardonable sin is inadvertence,
of not being alert, not quite awake."
—Joseph Campbell

The rabbit hole went straight on like a tunnel for some way, and
then dipped suddenly down, so suddenly that Alice had not a
moment to think about stopping herself before she found herself
falling down what seemed to be a very deep well.
—Chapter One,
Alice's Adventures in Wonderland

WHAT'S IN A NAME?

Romeo had a point about flowers. A rose by any other name would smell as sweet. But as he learned the hard way, people aren't flowers. Names and labels matter. They are symbols. Websites list thousands of monikers and their meanings for prospective parents who hope the child will embody the traits the name describes. Topping the list in 2012: Emma—from the Hebrew for "universal." It reflects the hope for a child who is welcome wherever life takes them. People identify saints' names with their characteristics too.

St. Christopher and St. Patrick were the only two I knew. The year I began teaching St. Christopher was demoted to local celebrations...sort of like Pluto losing planet status. How can that happen, I thought. Turns out he was getting too popular for his own good. He was in danger of becoming a cult. Not dangerous to him. Dangerous to the Church. It was my first glimpse into the strange workings of the Vatican—a secretive walled world that once wielded enormous power over more than a billion people.

Santa Monica is an ocean-front community surrounded on three sides by the City of Los Angeles. Founded by Gaspar de Portola on August 3, 1769, legend says it was named in honor of the feast day of Saint Monica, the mother of Saint Augustine, the most important figure in the ancient Western church.

Since 1939 Saint Monica's High School has occupied a site on Lincoln Avenue. It is two blocks from the Wilshire corridor stretching from beyond UCLA at one end to the Pacific Ocean at the other. Run by the Sisters of the Holy Names of Jesus and Mary, its mission is to "graduate students who demonstrate character, integrity, love of God, and others." The two-story buildings form a square around a paved central schoolyard. The parish church sits on one corner adjacent to the convent.

The school was reeling from the departure of nuns, priests, and brothers who left their orders in the halo of post-Vatican II optimism. In l965 there were an astonishing 180,000 women religious. By 2005 the number had dropped to 68,000.

Sister Jeanne, the department chair, wasn't anything like I imagined a nun. She was as cheerful in person as she sounded on the telephone. She wasn't fierce or mean-spirited like the ones that give rise to the "I Survived Catholic Schools" bumper stickers. Not isolated from the world. Not dour or judgmental. She was a shrewd, dedicated teacher with a heart as big as her wide girth.

She showed me the dusty supply room with its shelves of tattered books; how to operate the ditto machine without getting purple ink everywhere or suffer blinding headaches from the fumes; how to placate the more temperamental nuns. We spent little time on the curriculum "guidelines" since they didn't guide. Perfunctory and brief, they were sprinkled with words like "appreciate" and "understand." She was vague about the student newspaper, taking my high school experience as sufficient.

At the end of one meeting she said, "Did I mention the Monsignor?"

I didn't know what a monsignor was. I was afraid to ask. It sounded important. It must be a man. I knew that much about the church. I looked around, thinking he might appear on the spot. He didn't. I met him soon enough.

High school teachers either hate sophomores or love them. Their name, from the Greek *sophos*—wise, and *moros*—foolish, describes them to a T. The 1889 Century Dictionary says of sophomoric, "The exaggerated opinion which students this age have of their wisdom." The current Random House Dictionary goes farther: "childish, juvenile; tricky."

My assignment: five sophomore sections. I didn't have time to wonder about their name. I was elated. One prep! The number of course preparations is a bone of contention among teachers. Most prefer fewer. Maybe I got just one because I'm new, I thought. Later I learned it wasn't kindness or inexperience that motivated the sisters. Many people detest teaching sophomores. I inherited sections no one else wanted.

High school students recognize Lewis Carroll's Wonderland. Their worlds are the same. Both are full of strange words, inconsistencies, and the logical nonsense that reduces teachers to tears and Alice to ten inches in height as she begins her adventure. "What a curious feeling!" she says. "I must be shutting up like a telescope!" She eats a bit of cake, asking "Which way? Which way?" She expects to change one way or another. If she grows taller she'll be able reach the garden key on the glass table in the hall. If she shrinks she can slip under the door and follow the White Rabbit. She swallows the cake. Waits. She was surprised to find nothing happened. She didn't know what to do. Neither did I.

Saint Monica is revered for her piety and patience—patience with her arrogant, abusive husband, patience with her three children. Patient especially with her oldest son, Augustine, who experimented for 17 years before coming to Christianity.

When he did, his writing in *The Confessions* did more than any single document to bring the philosophy of the Greeks and the faith of early Christians together. His contemplation on the ability of language to both define man and to help him transcend the earth are among the most powerful discussions in Western thought.

Decades passed before I understood Augustine enough to include him in my teaching. I needed his mother's patience from the start. She is the patron saint of alcoholics, married women, and mothers. I was married, but that was the extent of my possible connection to her. I didn't consider my Protestant roots a problem. Saints have a bigger perspective. At least I hoped so.

I began "talking" to her as I walked home from school. How did she develop so much patience? How did she keep from giving up? What about my students? Most had been raised in religious schools. Why weren't they better behaved? Saint Monica never answered my questions, but in the twilight I sometimes felt her as I left campus. She was a soothing presence drifting on the ocean breeze curling through the quiet streets where I trudged along.

There are over 10,000 Catholic saints. Protestants have saints too. What they don't have is elaborate canonization processes with miracles attributed to individuals themselves, rather than in Christ's name.

Romeo would understand. Names weren't important to him either. Saints are people who have led holy, spiritual lives. Sister Jeanne was one. So was Saint Monica. Two Catholic women helping a Protestant. The labels didn't matter. To me. To them.

One was a model of perseverance. The other of practical solutions. I was lucky to have them both.

There were doors all round the hall, but they were all locked; and when Alice had been all the way down one side and up the other, trying every door, she walked sadly down the middle, wondering how she was ever to get out again.
—Chapter One,
Alice's Adventures in Wonderland

TIME INTERRUPTED

*T*he human brain is forever balancing its focus between task-oriented goals and daily interactions with the environment. Neuroscientists describe these two forms of attention as top-down (planning a strategy) and bottom-up (reacting to interruptions, like barking dogs). Our prefrontal cortex enables us to focus on what is important. When interruptions happen, scientists call it "performance impact."

Adam Gazzeley is an associate professor of neurology, physiology, and psychiatry at UC San Francisco. He says, "Multitasking is a myth. If you are doing more than one thing that requires your top-down resources, they will compete and conflict. Frequent distractions are a clear cost to performance."

Forget the lofty aspirations—foster new citizens, encourage democracy, create readers. Survival became my first-year goal. Questions loomed.

How to plan 50-minute classes? In first period I never got through lessons I struggled to design. By last period the same material took fifteen minutes. It was like living in Madeline L'Engle's *A Wrinkle in Time.*

How to cope with 35 different squirming, chattering teen-agers every hour? How could I stay organized? Everything conspired against me:

- Starting and stopping.

- Bargaining for the hall pass.
- Ringing bells.
- Surprising fire drills.
- Scurrying office messengers.
- Missing homework searches.
- Malfunctioning projectors.
- Whispering students doing homework for other classes.
- Searching for handouts I swore I brought with me.
- Neutralizing the siren call of the beach six tantalizing blocks away?

The tiny 10-point text font of *To Kill a Mockingbird* and the weighty tedium of *Warriner's Complete English Grammar* were irrelevant against the onslaught. So was I.

I was overwhelmed. Mystified. Mortified. After all, I had been IN high school not so long before. My teachers seemed calm and in control. We seemed pretty calm too. Bored maybe, but mellow. It was a long time before I understood being a good teacher takes tremendous effort, even when it doesn't look like it. I felt like a minor character in a chaotic 16th-century Pieter Brueghel painting. I couldn't decide if I was in "Large Fish Eat Small Fish" or "The Fight Between Carnival and Lent." Both fit.

In disgust I abandoned my "Tips for Classroom Management" list. I remember two. They were so ludicrous they are impossible to forget. The first: "IF a student is engaging in inappropriate behavior, move closer to them." That never worked.

Early on a boy brought a fountain pen adorned with a curvaceous bathing-suit-clad woman. When he turned the pen upside down the ink drained away, leaving her naked. Staccato laughter percolated from his corner of the room. Students snickered and pointed, passing the pen from hand to hand. I strode over to his desk. No one noticed. It was humiliating. I admitted what he was doing was more interesting than what I was doing. It was a clue.

The second instruction was worse. "NEVER raise your voice to get students' attention. Stand at the front of the room and they will quiet down shortly." Shortly? If I had continued with those helpful tips I would still be standing in Room 25 waiting. It was a clue. Not all instructions are worth following. Even when they come from experts. Maybe especially then.

In the spring of what had been a rocky year, things got worse. One April day I returned after lunch to find a man sitting in back of the classroom. At first I thought he was someone's father. Looking more closely, I saw matted stringy hair and a dirty khaki jacket. Not a parent. Students poured in, racing to beat the tardy bell. Normal chatter died as they spied the stranger.

I walked toward him. "May I help you?"

"I am waiting for God," he mumbled.

Well, I thought to myself, I am waiting for God too. This could be a long wait.

I smiled. "I see," I said. Of course I didn't see. I flipped through my meager mental store of strategies for unexpected events. Nothing.

"Could you wait outside?"

"No." Hunched over, he began tapping his fingers—a piano player without a piano. His pupils, dilated, darted back and forth like a trapped bird desperate to escape a closed room.

I began class as usual. The unusual things were the stranger's presence, the students' complete silence, and my shaking hand as I wrote on the board. I caught the eye of the boy nearest the door. He slipped out. The dean and two male teachers appeared. After some grappling, yelling, and an overturned desk the man was dragged away—shouting obscenities and screaming, "God, where are you?" The question hovered in the uncomfortable silence. My eyes rested on the crucifix beside the door. Where indeed? I wondered too.

It was a bad drug trip. Unbelievable as it seems, I returned to my grammar lesson as though nothing had happened. In that moment I lost the class forever. I am still embarrassed to think of what I could have done…honest dialogue for one thing. It was another clue on a path to a different kind of teaching.

But not that year. Interruptions overwhelmed me. No cerebral contortions could offset the reality of daily school life. Understanding has its own timetable, and comes when you're not looking for it. I was diligent about planning. I studied the textbooks every night, anticipating questions no one asked. Imagining discussions that didn't happen. Hoping for interest I never saw.

Alice had been close behind the White Rabbit when she turned the corner in the narrow passage down the rabbit hole, but the Rabbit was no longer to be seen. There was only the long, low hall, lit up by a row of lamps hanging from the roof, with all the doors locked. She wondered how she would get out. I wondered how I could get in.

We were both looking in the wrong place.

*"I wish I hadn't cried so much!" said Alice, as she swam about,
trying to find her way out. "I shall be punished for it now, I suppose,
by being drowned in my own tears! That will be a queer thing, to
be sure! However, everything is queer today."*
—Chapter Two,
Alice's Adventures in Wonderland

ANYWHERE BUT HERE

The worst class periods in the schedule. Afternoon.
Circadian rhythms sink. A toxic combination of too much
sugar, too little sleep, and too many people telling students what to
do for too long equals a recipe for disaster.

On a warm May day I dragged myself back to class after lunch.
I needed a nap. So did everyone else. What I found was the brown
metal wastebasket turned upside down on my desk. The morning's
trash—paper cups, candy wrappers, soda cans, half-eaten sandwiches,
apple cores, discarded assignments, used tissues, pencil sharpener
shavings—cascaded everywhere.

Frantic, I began scooping the trash back in the basket as the students
sauntered in, as though a teacher's desk that looked like a landfill was
an everyday occurrence. I remembered the lesson from my student-
teaching rotations: ignore behavior so you don't magnify it or worse,
alienate people. I started class without mentioning the mess behind me.

Conversations bubbled everywhere like steam from multiple
teapots. High school students carry on seamless conversations across
a classroom's farthest reaches. Separating students who talk to each
other is an exercise in futility. Today texting makes conversations
quieter. The attention problem remains.

My voice trailed off. Furious, frustrated, fed-up, I slammed the
chalk down. "This is a complete waste of time. You'd be better off at

the beach," I said through gritted teeth.

As if on cue, every student packed up and filed out. Room 25 was on the street side of the building. I flew to the window, tears streaming down my face. Standing on tiptoe I looked over the sill. A blue and white string of school uniforms sauntered down the sidewalk toward the ocean—as if it were the most natural thing in the world. In a beach city like Santa Monica, it was. But not in the middle of sixth period on a school day.

I stumbled across the quad to the principal's office. I burst in, sobbing. I ran past the astonished secretary. I knew my teaching career was over. Sister Michaeline Mary looked up as though hysterical people burst into her office often. (When I became a principal myself I realized that actually is true...but I didn't know then.) A tall, stately woman with a deceptively cherubic face and ramrod posture, her blue eyes twinkled through wire-rimmed glasses. White hair peeked out of her black veil—the last remnant of the habit the sisters discarded after Vatican II.

Sister Michaeline listened as I stumbled through my story, interrupting once to hand me a box of tissues. Finished, I slumped back in the chair across from her wide desk. Twisting the tissues into tiny shreds, I waited to be "dismissed." I heard stories of teachers let go, supposedly without cause. There is no tenure in Catholic schools. It is a reason some people who might otherwise be interested avoid them. In my 35 year career I never encountered a dismissal without cause. As an administrator I was part of two or three. They were painful, lengthy, and documented—just like public schools.

That was beside the point then. I was a probationary teacher in any system. The nun turned sideways in her swivel chair and gazed at the treetops peeking in through the windows. She sat motionless and silent. I thought I must have done something so awful she was speechless. Later I began to consider that perhaps, just perhaps, she had been talking to the God the man in the khaki jacket and I were both seeking.

At last she turned and leaned forward, resting her chin on her hands. "So, tell me Anne," she said, pausing between each word, "Do you really want to be a teacher?"

"Of course I do."

"Why are you willing to give up so quickly?"

"Quickly?!" I thought. The school year felt like a thousand days and it wasn't over.

"I'm not good at it," I moaned. "They aren't interested."

I rushed on, "Some days they cooperate—then they won't. I never can tell. Some days they act grown up. Then bam. They act worse than grade schoolers."

"Of course they do," she snapped. "They're sophomores."

With surprising grace for a woman so large, she rose, stepped around the desk and stood in front of me. I stood as well. My vision blurred as she studied my face. She was looking beyond my red eyes and tear-stained cheeks, to something I couldn't see myself.

"I'm not going to fire you," she said at last. "I do want you to spend more time with Sister Jeanne. Show her your lesson plans. Ask her questions. Spend time with us in the convent after school."

The convent? My eyes widened. A little smile tugged at the corners of her mouth. "I want you to get to know us. We're partners. You might be surprised what you learn."

"What if they don't come back?"

"They'll be back, and they'll expect a dean there lecturing them. I'll take any parent complaints. Ask Sister Jeanne how to handle the class."

As I turned to leave, she warned, "Don't use the dean. If they think you can't manage by yourself you will never be able to control them."

It was the best advice I ever received about classroom management. Year after year, in school after school, I saw tormented teachers depending on the deans. It never worked. It made things worse. Worse for the teachers and worse for the students whose focus became how long it would take before the tormented teacher would send for help. Private and public, wealthy and poor—the pattern existed everywhere.

I spent many afternoons in the convent the next year. It reminded me of sorority living. The retired sisters listened to my adventures and misadventures. They asked questions. Did you try this? Did you notice that? What would happen if you changed this? Why are you doing that? Is it important they learn what you're teaching? How will you know when they do?

The elderly nuns looked frail. They weren't. They were funny and more progressive than the parish community they served. They kept one veil on an entry table. When the bell rang they would jam it on their head and open the door. Veils aren't "one size fits all." They would laugh afterwards as the headpiece either perched like a tiny bird or slid down like a misshapen Zorro mask.

It was great education. Not about the science of an academic discipline. About the art and compassion of teaching. I began taking small steps toward the classroom I wanted to create.

A dozen years passed before I got close.

CHAPTER TWO

THE POOL OF TEARS

*Education is the ability to listen to almost anything without losing
your temper or your self-confidence.*
—Robert Frost

*Alice felt so desperate that she was ready to ask help of anyone: so,
when the Rabbit came near her, she began, in a low, timid voice, "If
you please Sir—" The Rabbit started violently, dropped the white
kid-gloves and the fan, and scurried away into the darkness, as
hard as he could go.*
—Chapter Two,
Alice's Adventures in Wonderland

LEND A HAND?

T eaching is a solitary affair. Once the door closes you are
on your own. Many teachers won't share, despite common
prep periods, in-service days, even team teaching. We all know
them. They're the people we studied with in college who left
with our notes before sharing theirs. Some things don't change.

After I moved to university jobs, I served as a Beginning Teacher
Support and Assessment (BTSA) coach for student teachers in local
public and private schools who needed help but couldn't find a volunteer on their own campus. A California program to try to keep

teachers from leaving in the first few years, BTSA struggled under the weight of the massive paperwork it required. Teachers are swamped. Even if they want to help they often can't.

Jon was a Yale graduate working in a large suburban public high school. Smart, enthusiastic, idealistic. Every week for a year we met to brainstorm. To celebrate successes. Troubleshoot problems. He grew into a popular, dynamic history teacher. After seven years he wrote to tell me he was leaving for a budget policy job in Sacramento. "I love teaching," he said. "I hate the isolation. My colleagues are invisible."

Richard Ingersoll is a researcher and Professor of Education and Sociology at the University of Pennsylvania. His work on teacher attrition reports nearly one-third of new teachers leave in the first three years. Half are gone by year five. Overall, the attrition rate is about 17 percent a year.

Jon was one of many left alone too soon to navigate the riptides of high school teaching. I capsized. The Holy Names didn't send a single person—they sent a community to the rescue. It made the difference.

Using the theater metaphor about teaching as "show time," I had allies in the wings as I worked the main stage. Most of the sisters are gone now. Their influence remains. Sister Michaeline never asked one question about my Protestant roots. Her compassion didn't stop at Protestants. It extended everywhere.

In spring 2012, evangelist Robert Schuller's famed Garden Grove Crystal Cathedral, with its 10,000 panes of glass and its cemetery, was sold in bankruptcy proceedings to the Catholic Diocese of Orange. Renamed Christ Cathedral, the Protestant landmark reopened in 2013 as the administrative and spiritual center for 1.2 million Catholics. Evangelicals are in an uproar. Some have family members or pre-paid crypts in what is now a "Catholic cemetery." They are horrified.

Reverend Schuller began preaching from the top of a snack bar in a closed drive-in theater in 1955. His motto was "Come as you are in the family car." At its peak, 20 million viewers around the world watched his televised "Hour of Power." Schuller's convenient "feel good" theology dismayed many denominations, including Catholics. They have their own reservations about taking over a building that could easily be a Disneyland attraction.

Christopher Smith, rector of the new church, says, "I just hope that we attend well to all the different people who are affected by this and also that this place be seen as a place where everyone is welcome to find hope and consolation and inspiration whether they are Catholic or not. That is the Bishop's desire—that we are a real credible witness to Christ in our world through our work here."

Teaching is better without labels. So is faith. I hope the Crystal Cathedral congregations, past and future, remember religion isn't about buildings. It never was.

The students who walked away from my classroom wore Catholic uniforms. I didn't think of them as Catholic students. They were our future.

Tomorrow needs everyone. Sister Michaeline knew. Reverend Smith knows. Some others, in every faith tradition, have forgotten.

For where two or three are gathered together in My name, there I am in the midst of them.
—Matthew 18:20

She got up and went to the table to measure herself by it, and found that, as nearly as she could guess, she was now about two feet high, and was going on, shrinking rapidly: she soon found out that the cause of this was the fan she was holding, and she dropped it hastily, just in time to save herself from shrinking away altogether.
—Chapter Two,
Alice's Adventures in Wonderland

From Monolith to Mosaic

Sitting on top of the desk, feet crossed like an Indian at a pow wow, the tousled blond teenager scowled. It was my first meeting with Kevin—the editor of the school paper. I was eager. He was grumpy.

"No one reads the newspaper," he said. "We can't write about important things. The Monsignor won't let us."

Skipping the monsignor part I said, "Is that the only problem?"

With a little coaxing he admitted, "Not really. Kids who sign up don't show up. We don't have a regular production schedule. The news is always old."

I may have been on shaky ground in the classroom but I was part of a good high school paper with a passionate faculty advisor. This challenge I could handle.

The newspaper was an after-school elective. The fifteen or so students had potential. I told them three things had to happen: quality writing, appealing layouts, and quicker turnaround from idea to distribution. They needed a model. It was time for a trip to the *Los Angeles Times*. All of them got the newspaper at home. None of them appreciated how good it was.

The *Times* has won more than 35 Pulitzer prizes in every category of journalistic excellence in a history dating to 1881. My favorite is their first. It was awarded in 1942 for public service for "confirming for all American newspapers the right of a free press as guaranteed under the constitution."

In 1965, four years before our tour, it became the first newspaper in history to publish over four million classified ads in one year. The students were awestruck by the massive production operation, the noisy linotype machines, and the roar of 900,000 tons of newsprint a year weaving back and forth along miles of presses like a gigantic loom. At 45,000 square miles, the circulation area was larger than Ohio. At one time, 1.5 million people from Santa Barbara to San Diego read the *Times* every day. Today the number is 770,000 and shrinking fast. In a desperate attempt to keep readers, the paper installed over 4,000 news racks that play music when they're opened. The first song: the theme from "Mission: Impossible."

On the bus ride home voices buzzed like bees around a hive. The students were inspired. Kevin leaned over to tell me the news. The staff decided the lead story was going to be condom use.

Sister Jeanne warned, "Run the condom story by the Monsignor."

Before Paul VI's reforms in 1968, there were at least fourteen "grades" of monsignor. It is an honorific title, loosely translated "my lord." He was the parish priest, and like most parish priests then, was charged with not just the pastoral duties (which is why most of them joined the priesthood) but also the oversight of the school and administration of his parish.

I made an appointment. Going to his office, it occurred to me not being Catholic has some advantages in Catholic schools. I thought of him as senior pastor, like Reverend Kirnahan, the father of one of my high school friends whose Methodist church I attended.

While the pastor analogy works, it doesn't take into account the weight of history behind the Catholic clergy. The church dates its beginning to the confession of Peter and the establishment of the church by Jesus. It is the world's oldest continuous institution. Besides, Protestant ministers don't wear black robes for daily office hours.

I was prompt. He gestured for me to sit across from him while he read my request. I passed the time counting the long row of buttons on his sleeve and admiring his wide colorful sash. Little glass boxes filled with bits of bones from dead saints sat on the bookcase behind him.

He began. "Parents want their children protected from our troubled world. The church is opposed," he paused for emphasis, "to birth control." Before I could respond he continued, "The topic is inappropriate for young innocents of the parish." Pushing the papers aside he finished, "Parents pay tuition. It funds your salary. Your job is to present the school in a positive light to the community, not get involved with social issues."

He punctuated his last comment with a wave. The meeting lasted five minutes.

Kevin's face fell when he heard the news. "Here's an idea," I said. "We can't make the condom story the lead. Why not make it your editorial subject?"

"Do you think we can?"

"If it is important to you and the staff, we have to," I said.

The monolith of church influence was cracking. The monsignor was caught in the confluence of trends that reshaped all society as the 20th century careened along. The traditional parochial school experience: Sunday services with your weekday classmates and their families, your school, church, and sports within a few blocks—simply, the parochial in parochial schools was disappearing. The school as an insular barrier separate from the world was no longer possible. It truth, it had never been possible. The world was there all along.

Month after month I went to the parish office. I began taking

Kevin. Sometimes the old priest approved the story list. Sometimes not.

In May the world exploded. There was one more meeting. The topic: Kent State.

Just then she heard something splashing about in the pool a little way off, and she swam nearer to make out what it was: at first she thought it must be a walrus or a hippopotamus, but then she remembered how small she was now, and she soon made out that it was only a mouse, that had slipped in like herself.
—Chapter Two,
Alice's Adventures in Wonderland

SINK OR SWIM

I t's an image for the ages. A young girl kneels over a dead body. Her arms are thrown out as she screams. The photograph won a Pulitzer Prize. The place—Kent State. The girl, a fourteen-year-old runaway named Mary Vecchio, says the day changed her life forever. It changed all of us.

On May 4, 1970, four students were killed and nine injured by the Ohio National Guard on the Kent State University campus during a protest of the American invasion of Cambodia. The Viet Cong had amassed a large stronghold along Cambodia's eastern border and were striking relentlessly at South Vietnamese and American troops on the other side. The shooting further polarized the country, already bitterly divided on the Vietnam War. Eight million high school and college students went on strike to protest the National Guard action.

Kevin, the student editor, came to see me. He brought Brian, a tiny, feisty redheaded staff writer, with him.

"We want to do reactions to Kent State for the last issue," Kevin said.

"We've got it mapped out," Brian interrupted. "We'll interview every group who reads the paper—students, teachers, parents."

"We'll identify them. We'll get different points of view," Kevin interjected. "We'll talk about the reasons the Guard was on campus. We'll find out what happened before the shooting."

Their plan was good. They anticipated objections they realized were coming. No matter.

Based on our experience, we expected the Monsignor to veto the idea.

I sought out Sister Jeanne. I found her sitting at a scarred wooden table in the deserted faculty workroom, grading papers. The afternoon sun filtered in, giving the room a sepia look. She listened. I waited. In the quiet I heard the wall clock "click-click" as each minute passed.

Sister Jeanne stacked her papers. "You know, Anne," she said, "sometimes it's easier to get forgiveness than permission. All Catholics know that. Now so do you." Without another word, she gathered her papers and lumbered out.

Kent State was the lead story in the final issue. I received the inevitable call to the parish office. I sent Kevin and Brian. The students had been fair and even-handed. The writing was crisp and accurate. Two student editorials took opposing views. Everywhere on campus people were reading the paper—the entire paper, not just the lead story. I continued advising the newspaper my second year at Saint Monica's. I was never called to the office again. Neither were they.

In journalism, as in all writing, every story is an invention, subject to the choices the writer makes. For the audience on the other side of the page, the words march forward with a certain inevitability—as if the story could exist one way only—the way it is written. But there is never one way to tell a story. Someone has chosen the beginning and the end. Each choice is made at the expense of an infinite number of variations. Who is to say which version is true?

The yearbook summarized the newspaper this way:

Current News and Controversial Views Make It a Great Year
for the Mariner

Under moderator Anne Koch and editor Kevin Weir, Mariner
'69-70 reached a turning point which proved to be favorable: a

*school paper which was current in its news and controversial in its
views. Many improvements were evident in the newspaper. Events
were reported in advance. In hopes of appealing to and retaining
the reader's interest, the paper was improved artistically. More
sports were included. Debatable topics were discussed. There was
even an astrological forecast; something for everyone. The editorial
section discussed such topics as apathy, the Vietnam War, drugs,
and problems on our campus. The biggest contribution from the
'new and now' Mariner was the link it created between the faculty
and students of awareness: the stepping stone to communication.*

There is no feeling quite as empty as a classroom when the final
bell rings in June. My first year was over. Success with the newspaper.
Failure in the classroom. As I straightened the desks for the last time
I wondered why the experiences were so different. I erased the board,
closed the blinds, and walked the short two blocks home.

Summer had come. I found another clue, but not in a classroom.
Under a tree. A chipmunk showed me.

CHAPTER THREE

THE CAUCUS RACE AND A LONG TALE

What we want to see is the child in pursuit of knowledge, and not knowledge in pursuit of the child.
—George Bernard Shaw

They were indeed a queer-looking party that assembled on the bank—the birds with draggled feathers, the animals with their fur clinging close to them, all dripping wet, cross, and uncomfortable.
—Chapter Three
Alice's Adventures in Wonderland

FAIRIES IN THE MIST

The way forward is paradoxically to look not ahead, but to look around," said John Seely Brown, former Director of the Xerox Palo Alto Research Center and co-author of *The Social Life of Information*. Brown and his research colleague Paul Duguid were speculating on the tunnel-ahead approach of technologies that drive people to think if we focus hard enough on information, we can get where we want to go most directly.

In their 2000 book they argued the fuzzy stuff around the edges—context, background, history, common knowledge, social resources—

is not as irrelevant as it seems. It provides balance and perspective. It holds alternatives. Offers breadth of vision. Indicates choices. Helps clarify purpose and meaning. They concluded it is only with the help of what lies beyond that any sense can be made of the information at hand. I knew they were right. It was a lesson I learned not in a research lab, but outdoors, 30 years earlier.

A change of scenery. After the whirlpool of high school teaching and the pressure of Jim's doctoral program, a chance for summer work in Yellowstone National Park was the escape we needed. He ran the Concessioners' Recreation Program for 3000 summer-worker college students. I edited the park newspaper. The Yellowstone Cub had a circulation of 2000, and a "pass on" readership about the same. I was the sole employee.

Yellowstone was 1100 miles from Los Angeles. In reality, it was farther. The city's population was in excess of two million people. West Yellowstone boasted 1500 in the summer. Los Angeles County is a prickly sprawl, gripping more than 4700 square miles. Yellowstone is a third smaller—a gentle blanket resting across vast open spaces. The city's bright lights made day and night indistinguishable. The park's lights—sun and stars—separated time.

Urban life was intense—harsh, hostile, hassled. Edgy. Andy Warhol art, political assassinations on everyone's mind, the constant drone of automobiles, the sloppy fashion of hippie chic. Pundits suggested we should change our national symbol from the bald eagle to the zebra—black and white stripes, never to connect. The stress oozed into the schools—insidious, subtle, wily. A hard place to teach. A hard place to learn.

I wondered. Would an angry world change Yellowstone? It wasn't the right question. People may change it on the surface, but not its soul. It changes them. It changed me. What I thought about beyond the rigid format of lesson plans. It was a transformation fueled by where we lived, who we worked with, what I saw around me.

We set up house near Mammoth Hot Springs in a tiny, shabby, dusty two-room cabin with uneven wood floors. A porch sagged around two sides like a wilted shirt collar. We shared the space with a parade of mice, spiders, strange flying bugs, and a large moose who positioned himself more than once between the porch and our parked 1967 Chevrolet.

The warm springs bubbled a hundred yards away. The sulphur created a yellow mist with a greenish tinge, a smell like rotten eggs, and a temperature that approached 300 degrees. It was easy to imagine Macbeth's witches squatting nearby. When we weren't working we sat on the porch—the only place there weren't mice. There were no other cabins nearby, few tourists in the remote spot, no familiar sounds. The silence was deafening. As my hearing improved I realized it wasn't silent—it was different. Creatures communicating with one another in combinations like an Appalachian hill band. Reminding us we were visitors. Inviting us to pay attention. I wondered. Had I listened to my students?

Employee talent shows revealed a wide array of skills. By day park visitors saw laundry workers, desk clerks, housekeepers, gas station attendants, fishing guides, stable hands, cafeteria employees. By night they transformed into French horn players, pianists, folk singers, dancers, puppeteers, and thespians. The Mammoth employees staged their own version of Thornton Wilder's play, "Our Town," updating every scene by two decades. The opening scenes were set in 1890—the closing scenes in the future.

Artists and scientists both know time is a social construct. Watching the play reminded me. Where had I so hurriedly been dragging my students? Why? My classroom had been like the racecourse the Dodo set up to dry the creatures who fell in the pool of tears. The course was sort of a circle, with no particular destination. The animals began running when they liked, and left off when they liked, so it was not easy to know when the race was over, how long it was, who had won.

Half the world's geothermal features are in Yellowstone—more than 10,000 geysers, including Old Faithful (which erupts about 20 times a day), hot springs, and mud pots. A World Heritage Site since 1978, it remains a majestic true wilderness—97 percent undeveloped.

In 1806 John Colter, a member of the Lewis and Clark expedition, broke off to join fur trappers. He saw the geothermal pools but dismissed them as delirium brought on by a recent encounter with Blackfoot Indians. As I gazed across the mists at sunset, I began to see delicate shadows form and re-form. Ideas flitted by. Park images and my first year students mingled in strange ways.

The cabin no longer seemed so shabby. The students not so detached. They were engaged with each other—if not with me. Our languages were different. It was like the conversation among the wet animals drying off at Wonderland's pool.

> *"The patriotic archbishop of Canterbury, found it advisable—"*
> *said the Mouse.*
> *"Found what?" said the Duck;*
> *"Found it," the Mouse replied rather crossly: "of course you know*
> *what 'it' means."*
> *"I know what 'it' means well enough, when I find a thing," said*
> *the Duck: "it's generally a frog, or a worm. The question is, what*
> *did the archbishop find?"*

The Mouse didn't notice the question. His story didn't dry off the animals or Alice. Hadn't I done the same thing? Wrong approach. Bad timing.

As I looked into the mists of Yellowstone day after day, I began to see a new way to be in the world. More imaginative. More flexible. And when the light was just right at dusk I caught glimpses of fairies—those unique magic creations as old as time. Creatures who don't live by human rules. Who live in a world of exquisite delight, enchanted danger, and wonder. I didn't forget them when I returned to school.

I brought them with me.

"And who is Dinah, if I might venture to ask the question?"
said the Lory.
"Dinah's our cat. And she's such a capital one for catching mice, you
can't think! And oh, I wish you could see her after the birds!
Why, she'll eat a little bird as soon as look at it!"
This speech caused a remarkable sensation among the party.... On
various pretexts they all moved off, and soon Alice was left alone.
—Chapter Three,
Alice's Adventures in Wonderland

You See WHAT?

West New York is a New Jersey city across the Hudson from Manhattan. In July 2012, someone reported seeing the Virgin Mary in a Ginkgo biloba tree in the center of a city best known for its high crime rate and depressed economy. Wire services reported large flocks of Catholics gathering to observe the vision. People interested. Intrigued. Inspired.

Not that there is anything unique about what people saw. Both Mary and Jesus pop up in odd places. Several years ago the *Miami Herald* reported a woman in Port St. Lucie, Florida, saw him in a cell-phone picture on her TV screen. A woman in Clermont saw him in a power meter. In Houston, Chyanna Richards reported seeing the image of Christ in a splotch of green mold on the wall above her tub. A couple in Anderson County, South Carolina, saw him on a Walmart receipt.

In high school a shy classmate invited me to her Nazarene church because, she said, "You'll be able to see the image of a pillar of salt (Genesis 19:26) in the beveled window on the side of the building."

I went. All I saw was sun glancing through the glass. That doesn't mean she and others didn't see what they said they saw. It only means I didn't.

As the sole employee of the Yellowstone Park newspaper I recruited stringers from the student employee ranks, sold ads, designed layouts on a big wooden table in the back of the recreation center, delivered papers to racks and employee dorms, wrote copy, and took pictures with a boxy black Polaroid camera I carried everywhere.

Navigating the narrow roads crowded with some of the 100,000 people who visit the park every year, stopped traffic was normal as tourists flung their car doors open and swarmed away from their vehicles—cameras swinging from their necks like alien oversized I.D. tags. I always hopped out, hoping for an interesting shot. Bear cubs? Deer? More often than not, it was chipmunks.

One day, bored while I waited, I took pictures of tourists taking pictures of Disney's Alvin and friends. I squinted through the small square on top of the box, shifting it up and down in frustration. I wanted the tall people and the small rodents in the same frame. Where should I concentrate? It was tricky. Photographers who use viewfinder cameras with no adjustable focusing system talk about "the parallax problem." It is a difference of orientation of an object viewed along two lines of sight.

For example, in looking at moving objects, those in the distance move more slowly than those close to the camera. This is because the viewer is just above the lens, so what you see and what the camera sees are slightly different. As I squinted through the Polaroid day after day it dawned on me my teaching had only one perspective, and it wasn't mine. It wasn't the students'. The Teacher's Manual chose what was important. The ready-made lessons were a lifeline as I thrashed about in a sea of unfamiliar people and mountains of paper. The problem… they didn't work.

Chipmunks aren't bears, but if you live in cement cities seeing a small furry creature watching you might be a connection you need. Developing Polaroid pictures requires the photographer to pull the pack film out of the camera after each shot, wait a couple of minutes, and separate the positive and negative papers. The negatives were as interesting as the photos. Their reversed light and shadow allowed different shapes to appear. Minor features dominated. The primary subject receded. Composition shifted.

Studying both the pictures and negatives of excited tourists snapping away, a thought drifted into view like a wispy cloud on a flat blue sky. What do students focus on when they read assignments? What is important to them? I used the tourist/chipmunk shot in an article about park "residents" greeting guests. I expected comments about how boring the image was. Instead, the pictures generated more positive feedback than any of bears I ran.

Fall came. The first year I seated students alphabetically, passed out the course outline and then read it to them. I moved on to class rules, school rules, dress code rules, permission to leave class rules, homework rules, make-up rules, forms for parents to sign. I did all the talking. I had no idea who I was talking to. By the end of the day my voice was a barely audible croak.

The second year I told students to sit anywhere, but stay there until I learned their names. I changed their seats every month. Classrooms look different from different angles too. I took roll. I studied their faces. I asked other students to repeat names they just heard, row by row.

I passed out 3x5 cards. "Write your name. Under it write what you prefer to be called. Then write one thing we wouldn't know about you if you didn't tell us." My goal was to learn their names and for them to learn each other's names. Five periods is a challenge. Names are critical. Anonymous people are disengaged. Without a name they don't care. They don't need to.

"What do you do in English classes?" I asked.

Silence. Smug sidelong glances. Someone would volunteer, "Read."

"That's part of it," I said. "Let's get started."

"We don't have our books yet," they countered.

"You won't need them."

I passed out a 16th century graphic by Pieter Bruegel the Elder. An artist and designer, his paintings are famous for pointing out the follies of man—something teenagers see around them every day. The graphic is full of chaotic images—raging seas, prisons, wrecked boats, burning houses. In the middle a tall, calm woman stands on a large anchor. She holds a spade in one hand, a scythe in the other. On her head is a beehive.

"Work with someone else. Introduce yourselves. Write down what you see. Come up with a title."

"This isn't reading," every class protested.

"This is exactly what reading is."

The room hummed. I listened. I began to learn about them. Students began to learn about each other. I didn't lose my voice. They wrote the tentative titles and their names on large poster sheets and stapled the notes to the bottom like fringe on a giant white shirt. Chaos—Sadness—Loss—Fear—were among their choices.

It was a start. We came back to the picture several times the first week. I talked about the artist, about the times in which he lived. We looked for clues. They added more and more to what they saw. After some heated debates, students agreed the oversized woman in the center was the key. They called her Peace and agreed on a final title—"Peace Amid Despair." They supported the choice in the first writing assignment. Bruegel called his picture HOPE. The student title worked just as well.

The animals desert Alice as she dries off after the caucus race. She doesn't understand their point of view. After all, she thinks, she was only talking about her cat. "I wish I hadn't mentioned Dinah," she said to herself in a melancholy tone. "Nobody seems to like her down here, and she's the best cat in the world."

Her cat may be wonderful. Talking about her isn't if your conversation is with a mouse or a bird. Audience matters. She was learning. So was I.

It would be simple and easy to make fun of people who see Mary and Jesus in bathrooms and tree trunks. Easy to ridicule tourists for driving hundreds of miles to photograph chipmunks. Easy to use pre-packaged lessons. Easy to blame their failure on students. I was a fan of H.L. Mencken, the journalist and writer. How did I forget his caustic observation, "For every complex problem there is an answer that is clear, simple, and wrong."

Bill Cain is a Jesuit priest who won a Peabody Award for a short-lived television series about the complexity of faith in the modern world. In one episode his main character, Father Ray, asked: "Which man is truly crazy, the one who hears thunder and thinks it is the voice of God, or the one who hears the voice of God and thinks it's only thunder?"

I spent the summer calibrating, checking, changing my camera focus. I captured more interesting images. My eyesight improved. So did my insight. It's true that seeing is believing, but believing is also seeing.

I wondered. Perhaps sometimes there is no difference between the two.

*"Ahem!" said the Mouse with an important air. "Are you all ready?
This is the driest thing I know. Silence all round, if you please!
'William the Conqueror, whose cause was favored by the pope, was
submitted to by the English, who wanted leaders..."'
"Ugh!" said the Lory, with a shiver.*
—Chapter Three,
Alice's Adventures in Wonderland

Yesterday's Model

It was a cheerful note card from my "southern cousins," as my Los Angeles relatives call themselves. The cover was a photo of a restored rural schoolhouse. A lectern stood at the left side, the American flag behind it. A teacher's desk occupied the front middle. In the right corner a straight-back chair sat alone, a tall dunce cap sitting on the seat. Rows of wooden desks, their iron legs bolted to the floor, filled the room. They looked like an Army platoon at attention. The blackboard proclaimed,

MASON STREET SCHOOL
BUILT 1865
Building is 85 percent original

Mason Street was one of the first elementary schools in California and the first in San Diego County. It is a museum now in Old Town, San Diego's Historic Park. I had visited it many times. There was an iron stove and water bucket out of the picture's view. The school was free and open to everyone. Their first teacher, Mary Chase Walker, was paid $65 a month. She left after eleven months to get married.

Even without the details, we'd all know what we were looking at. A schoolroom. A room that still exists. Despite the radical changes since Mason was built, schools are one of the few places that remain recognizable. They looked like factories then. They look like factories now. Because they are. I knew what Mason Street produced. What about today's schools? I wonder.

The Industrial Revolution changed society. There were trade-offs. People left farms for opportunities in cities. Parents no longer worked at home. School became the primary mechanism between life in family and life as an adult. In his 1968 book, *On What Is Learned in School*, sociologist Robert Dreeben wrote that schools teach children to function in the modern world: to be independent and take responsibility, to recognize we are all part of a group, and that when exceptions are made they are made fairly.

I took the Dreeben book to Yellowstone. His credentials were impressive.

Harvard Ph.D., chair of Department of Education at the University of Chicago, widely respected. In theory he is right. In practice the schools I worked in didn't deliver. They couldn't. The Industrial Age morphed into a brave new world—a world where students remain dependent on parents until they approach 30, according to most sociologists. Technology has led to a culture of the self—self-creation, self-promotion, self-referential. Worst, behavioral exceptions—in finance, in sports, even in law—are not made fairly.

O.J. Simpson is one example. We knew an attorney who was part of the defense team that worked on Simpson's acquittal. Years later I asked him if he felt the decision was right. He stared at me. "The law isn't about right and wrong," he said. "It's about strategy."

As a young teacher, with none of the professional education I later acquired, I didn't know what was wrong in my classroom—just that something was. Schools were noisy, hurried. Clocks everywhere. Activity was the order of the day. The national parks offered a change— quieter, slower. There were clocks, but not on every tree. Could I take some of that atmosphere back to school? I wondered.

Laying out the park newspaper for an early June issue, I decided rather than the conventional front page news design, I would try something different—a large waterfall image with John Muir's words underneath: "I found a land of beauty I never would have known… A land that God had made and man had left alone."

A summer worker taking a break in the recreation center looked at the layout. "I'm a journalism major," he said. "The front page is for important news. You should move that to page three."

"This is important news," I countered. "It's the most important idea they'll read this week."

I returned to the city convinced the factory model wasn't the answer. The old approach didn't work. Albert Einstein knew that. He said, "We can't solve problems by using the same kind of thinking we used when we created them." I wasn't skilled enough to individualize lessons for each student. I wouldn't have a job if I let them study only what interested them.

I could do two things I learned from the rangers. First, start with student questions. Second, use their vocabulary. New teachers, insecure and either not much older than their charges or "career switchers" who were used to particular workplace vocabularies, often overwhelm students with everything they know about a topic, using every vocabulary word they ever encountered. I was guilty, and I had a big vocabulary.

I could almost hear the animals scolding Alice, dazed and confused early in her Wonderland adventure. "Speak English!" said the Eaglet. "I don't know the meaning of half those long words, and, what's more, I don't believe you do either!"

At the end of my second teaching year, my husband accepted a job at the University of Oregon. I had just begun figuring out what being a teacher meant. I tucked the lessons away, said goodbye to the palm trees, the statue of Saint Monica at the front of the church, the wide Pacific almost at my classroom door. We were leaving a place we both loved for a new life—far from family, friends, familiar sites. Growing up in the Navy was good preparation. I knew what writer Katherine Anne Porter says is true, "Win or lose, life doesn't begin on the first try."

Neither does teaching.

Part Two

CALCULATE AND CONNECT

WHAT DO YOU KNOW?

Though it often seems hard to believe, instructors are frequently asked to build courses to teach people what they already know or to use instruction to solve problems that can't be solved by instruction.
—Robert F. Mager

CHAPTER FOUR

THE RABBIT SENDS IN A LITTLE BILL

Children, like animals, use all their senses to discover the world.
—Eudora Welty

"Oh, you foolish Alice!" she answered herself. "How can you learn lessons in here? Why there's hardly any room for you, and no room at all for any lesson books!"
—Chapter Four,
Alice's Adventures in Wonderland

GROWING PAINS

What happens to people when their life or their society transforms into something new and unexpected?

In summer 2012, a neuroscience doctoral student, James Holmes, dyed his hair orange and opened fire in a crowded movie theater on opening night of "The Dark Knight" in Aurora, Colorado. Twelve people were killed. Fifty-eight injured. Why? After all the psychological tests, biographical searches, interviews, we still won't know. People will offer a circular argument: "He must have been mad to do it, and he did it because he was mad." Nature drives us to seek explanation and understanding.

Are the answers found in schools? Some are. More are not.

Anxious to stay engaged in some outside activity in Oregon, I took a preschool teaching job. I knew I wouldn't learn anything, but I would earn pocket money. I was right about the money. Wrong about the learning. I watched teachers use their considerable skill to plan multiple activities for every 20-minute segment of a three-hour class of three- and four-year-olds. I was humbled by their talent and creativity. We spent more time preparing than we did executing. Years later I drew on those experiences to craft the 90-minute high school blocks or four-hour university graduate classes I taught. Woodrow Wilson said, "If I am to speak ten minutes, I need a week for preparation… if an hour, I am ready now." The same is true for lesson planning no matter the age group.

Alice grows more confident as she searches for the garden. She is learning. Not from her schoolbooks. From the challenges she faces. From slowly figuring out Wonderland. When she sends the little lizard Bill up the chimney with one sharp kick she is growing braver, more skilled, more socially savvy in the strange world she is navigating. So was I. Two dozen four-year-olds doing water table, play dough, dress-up, cooking, and hamster races at five different stations at the same time will do that.

Ten years away from high school. Ten years of missing teenagers. We returned to California. My affection for the Holy Names nuns convinced me I wanted to be in a healthy Catholic school. They embodied Buckminster Fuller's idea, "God is a verb." I wanted to work in a school where questions were encouraged, where religion was discussed, where prayer was allowed, where people didn't apologize for their faith. They lived it. The Catholic hierarchy isn't encouraging, but many of its American religious orders are.

The single biggest lesson from my years away from high school was that some things don't have answers, or at least a single answer. An atrocious event like the Aurora massacre brings us against something most of us ignore: our longing for explanation exceeds our grasp. It always will. We seek answers even where there may be none. It is like Haitian peasants say, "Behind mountains, more mountains."

It's still worth looking. Voltaire said, "All men are born with a nose and ten fingers, but no one was born with a knowledge of God."

Catholic schools are one place to look…and learn.

Alice looked all around her at the flowers and the blades of grass, but she could not see anything that looked like the right thing to eat or drink under the circumstances. There was a large mushroom growing near her, about the same height as herself; and, when she had looked under it, and on both sides of it, and behind it, it occurred to her that she might as well look and see what was on top of it.

She stretched herself up on tiptoe, and peeped over the edge of the mushroom, and her eyes immediately met those of a large blue caterpillar, that was sitting on the top, with its arms folded, quietly smoking a long hookah, and taking not the smallest notice of her or of anything else.
—Chapter Four,
Alice's Adventures in Wonderland

ELEPHANTS AND GORILLAS

A handsome blond graduate student popped his head over a cubicle in the Development Office at Santa Clara University as I walked through the building several years ago. "Mrs. Koch," he called. "Do you remember me from high school?"

I stared, willing my mind backward. It felt like Mark Twain's line, "The space-annihilating power of thought," in his essay "From Bombay to Missouri":

"For just one second all that goes to make the me in me was in a Missourian village, vividly seeing pictures of fifty years ago…and in the next second I was back in Bombay."

I couldn't dig out his name, but there was a clear mental picture of a varsity soccer player, resting his foot on a ball, staring glumly at an empty exam book. My mind slipped backward. I remembered the scene.

"Why aren't you writing?" I asked.

He looked up. "Because I didn't read. I listen. I never read. You didn't go over the exact questions you were going to ask," he said in an aggrieved voice.

"It's not an exact question, but you can do it. Relax. Think about you. Your reactions to the plays. Do you see yourself in one? Someone you know? You have two days in class. I guess you'll have to read tonight."

I refocused. There he was, 15 years later, clutching a worn paperback copy of collected Arthur Miller plays. "Wow. I can't believe you're here," he said.

Hurrying around his cubicle he wrapped me in a one-armed hug. With his other hand he waved a book under my nose. "Look! I had to read something optional for a class. I remembered this Miller collection. This time I read."

"Nice work. Tell me what you learned this time."

"Now?"

"Of course. Books change every time we read them because we change."

"Well," he said. "For one thing you don't have to be a great person in the classic sense to have a tragic life. Willy Loman is an example."

Twenty minutes later we were still talking about "Death of a Salesman."

"Wish I could talk more" he said, looking at the wall clock above his cube. "I've gotta go. I'm on a club soccer team."

Some things change. Some stay the same. I'm glad.

Elephants in the room. Classrooms. Family rooms. Everywhere. Those difficult problems no one talks about. For schools, the reality that most students don't read, even if they know how, is an elephant. In 2006 a British artist, Banksy, set the phrase in visual form in a Los

Angeles exhibit. In a room he featured a large colorful pachyderm covered in the same design as the wallpaper behind him. A woman sat on a couch reading. Was she unaware the elephant was there, or unwilling to acknowledge it?

Alice Liddell was the real-life Victorian little girl for whom *Alice's Adventures in Wonderland* was written. Above the ground were clear answers, clear roles, clear expectations for everything from behavior to school curricula. Her creator, a deacon and mathematics lecturer at Oxford's Christ Church College, was as two-sided as the Wonderland tale.

Carroll's real name—Charles Lutwidge Dodgson. In his academic work, he invented ciphers, designed puzzles centering on words and numbers, studied logical paradoxes. Wonderland is an inspired fantasy tale. It is also a satire on Victorian pomposity and rigidity. Lessons real Alice learned at school weren't helpful in her Wonderland dream. We're still teaching some of the same lessons. They are still not helpful. We still don't acknowledge the fact. Elephants.

Lewis Carroll wasn't alone in satirizing 19th-century conventional thinking. In Charles Dickens' 1854 novel *Hard Times*, he introduces a schoolmaster, Thomas Gradgrind, in a chapter ominously titled "Murdering the Innocents."

The scene was a plain, bare, monotonous vault of a schoolroom, and the speaker's square forefinger emphasized his observations by underscoring every sentence by poking the schoolmaster's sleeve. "In this life, we want nothing but Facts, sir; nothing but Facts!"

The speaker, and the schoolmaster, and the third grown person present, all backed up a little, and swept with their eyes the inclined plane of little vessels then and there arranged in order, ready to have imperial gallons of facts poured into them until they were full to the brim.

"Thomas Gradgrind, sir. A man of realities. A man of facts and calculations. A man who proceeds upon the principle that two and two are four, and nothing over and who is not to be talked into allowing for anything over. With a rule and a pair of scales, and the multiplication table always in his pocket, sir, ready to weigh and measure any parcel of human nature, and tell you exactly what it comes to."

Schools struggle to shape education to better fit today's world and today's students. Facts are important. When they are the single measure of education they create elephants. We're measuring. We're not teaching. We're pretending.

As a curriculum coordinator I participated in performance evaluations of fellow teachers. Sometimes a vice-principal joined us. After one the administrator said, "It wasn't bad but there should be a quiz everyday to check for understanding."

If it takes a quiz every day for a teacher to tell if students understand, we have bigger problems than fact measurement. Facts alone disconnected from thinking masquerade as achievement. We're wasting time. Our time—their time. They won't tolerate it for long. They disconnect. Then we have not just an elephant but also a gorilla in the room. We become invisible to one another.

In 2010 Harvard researchers Chris Chabris and Dan Simons wrote *The Invisible Gorilla* about their work on perception and cognitive illusions. In their now-famous experiment six people, three with white shirts and three with black shirts, are passing a basketball around. Subjects were directed to count how many times the white shirts passed the ball. Midway through the video a man in a gorilla suit walks through the game, stops for nine seconds, and then walks off. More than half the participants in the study didn't even see him. The conclusion: we miss a lot and, worse, we don't know we're missing it.

When I returned home I rummaged in the garage to find the old exam my former student had struggled to begin. It read:

FAMILY RELATIONSHIPS in one Arthur Miller play.
THE PROCESS: Spend a day creating a TEXT-BASED brain-
storm. Spend a second day creating a map linking your text
choice. From the pattern you create develop a one-sentence thesis.
THE OBJECTIVES:
Analysis and synthesis around this topic.
The chance to create and recognize the
 difference between initial text search/final product.
THE EVALUATION:
Demonstrates both objectives.
Thesis supported by YOUR text choices.
THE TOOLS:
Open book.
Open notes.
Your brain. Do this by yourself.
THE ADVICE: Consider. Create. Choose. Think. Think again.

No elephants. No gorillas. Just people sense-making.

Time is the problem. It is as disinterested in us as the long blue caterpillar Alice spies smoking a hookah on the mushroom near her. Some students don't have 15 more years.

It's a lesson I wish I hadn't learned.

*As soon as she was small enough to get through the door, she ran
out of the house, and found quite a crowd of little animals and
birds waiting outside. The poor little Lizard, Bill, was in the middle,
being held up by two guinea pigs… They all made a rush at Alice
the moment she appeared; but she ran off as hard as she could, and
soon found herself safe in a thick wood.
'Oh dear! I'd nearly forgotten that I've got to grow up again. Let me
see—how is it to be managed?*
—Chapter Four,
Alice's Adventures in Wonderland

Unknown Unknowns

The 1964 New York World's Fair theme was "Man's Achievements in an Expanding Universe." For a high school junior, with tomorrow "just around the corner," as teachers kept telling us, it was a dazzling glimpse of the future—our future. There were exhibits for atomic power, cars that drove themselves, domed cities under sea and in outer space, and people traveling by jetpack. There was nothing about the Internet, personal computers, smart phones, or wireless communication.

This wasn't a surprise to the University of Pennsylvania's Professor Phillip Tetlock, who a few years ago examined 27,451 predictions by 284 historians, scientists, and futurists. He found they were wrong more than 50 percent of the time—worse than if they had flipped a coin. Even the smartest people are prone to oversimplifying the world and overestimating the idea that knowledge leads to right answers to complicated questions.

Victor's smile was the first thing people noticed. It lit up his dark eyes. It lit up the room. He was a friendly, soft-spoken sophomore. He didn't see social groups. He saw people. A swimmer, he had his heart set on the Air Force Academy. By his senior year he had taken almost every course I taught. When he enrolled in Advanced Placement he came to see me.

"No matter what grades I earn, I want the chance to rewrite every assignment for no credit if I don't do well. Is that okay?" he said.

His cheerful face was uncharacteristically serious. "I want to learn everything I can. I'm pretty sure I'm going to get an Academy appointment, and I want to be ready."

"I'm willing if you are."

Victor kept his word. He never asked for grade changes. Most of his work was excellent anyway. Even so, he would often end up in the classroom on his way to the pool, waving a timed writing in his hand and saying, "I think this sounds weak, Mrs. Koch. Don't you?"

"Maybe. But it's only a drill."

"Every drill counts. I'll do it over."

I spent many extra hours with Victor. Friends joined him. Students from other classes. His leadership and personality drew people to him and to things that mattered to him. Excellence mattered. He inspired others by being himself.

His class went to two local theater productions. "Out of one box and into another," I said. Early in the course they saw Lillian Hellman's "Toys in the Attic." I showed them the 1957 *New York Times* interview she gave before its premier. "I wanted to say that not all kinds of love are noble and good, that there is much in love that is destructive, including the love that holds up false notions of success, of the acquisition of money," she said.

Students debated success and money for hours. Victor was impatient. "They're not related," he said. "Success is more complicated. Money isn't. It's a way to do something that matters. People mess it up."

Later they saw Sam Shepard's "True West"—a play about heroism and the question, "When the frontier goes, where does the pioneer spirit go?"

After both plays Victor was energized. He wrote reflections I didn't even assign.

He thought "True West" asked an easy question.

"There's always a frontier," he wrote. "Look up!"

The summer day before he left for Colorado Springs he appeared at my home. I wrote my address on the board the first day of every year. "If you need help, here I am," I said. Many students took me up on it. Victor was one. That day he carried a bouquet of flowers, a blue and white Air Force Academy pennant, a huge smile, and a card. It read:

> *Dear Mrs. Koch, I wouldn't be going to Colorado without your love and encouragement these last three years. Remember my yearbook quote: "Don't walk in front of me. I may not follow. Don't walk behind me. I may not lead. Walk beside me and be my friend." Thanks for being my friend and teacher. I'll send you my papers (the good ones, anyway!) I won't forget you. Aim High! Love, Victor*

School began again. Before the first assembly the intercom crackled on. The principal announced they had just received word that a DLS graduate, Victor Nigro, had collapsed and died at the Air Force Academy while playing tennis. Over the years De La Salle has lost a number of students. Rarely were they announced without prior notice to the faculty. I leaned my head against the blackboard. The door flew open. The teacher next door burst in.

"You're coming with me," he said. Turning to the class, he barked, "Stay put."

Grabbing my arm, he strode down the hall to the Director of Studies. Her door was shut. Not bothering to knock, he barged in.

Taking one look at me, she ground out her cigarette and grabbed her keys. "Let's go."

She drove me to the Nigro home. I had never been there, but it was the place I needed to be. I hadn't said a single word since the intercom. The best Catholic schools are an enormous family. Like any family they are sources of worry, frustration, and disappointment. They are also sources of love and support. Victor was part of that family. My colleague and director knew that. He was part of their family too. I spent the rest of day at the Nigro kitchen table, lost in despair, mixing my tears with theirs.

At Victor's funeral mass, one speaker quoted the words Ronald Reagan had used the year before when the Challenger space shuttle exploded 74 seconds after lift-off. The explosion and swirling smoke trails were broadcast over and over on campus television. The President said, "We will never forget them, nor the last time we saw them, this morning, as they prepared for their journey, waved goodbye and 'slipped the surly bonds of earth to touch the face of God.'"

I will never forget Victor either. Grief reminds you how much you invest in people you love. His parents gave me his Academy papers. Among them was a letter from his English instructor. It said in part,

> *I want to offer you my remembrance of Victor. He was a special person and a good student, and I miss him. Victor turned in his journal on 14 September, as requested by me. I was disappointed with the performance of the class overall, but Victor's work was clearly better than the rest. One of the things that impressed me is he did follow-ups. An example is his entry on Annie Dillard, where he followed up on 14 September his thoughts that he began on 11 September. That's one of the things that identified Victor as a serious student, one who enjoyed learning, one who was a good writer. This attitude was also obvious from his habit of asking*

questions almost every day after class. I just wanted you to know that I miss the questions, and I miss the sheepish grin.

Sincerely,
John M. Thomson Major USAF

Anton Chekhov wrote, "There ought to be a man with a hammer behind the door of every happy man, to remind him by his constant knocks…that life will sooner or later show him its claws…sickness… poverty…loss." Much of what the 1964 World Fair envisioned hasn't happened. In reality there are so many variables in human affairs and in the natural world we can only see what's directly ahead of us, and even then not very well. We can't anticipate what Donald Rumsfeld called "the unknown unknowns."

My grief about Victor has never completely disappeared. Grief doesn't. It leaves an ache that flares up at the most unexpected times. The prediction we can count on about the future: When it comes banging on the door, we will be surprised.

I couldn't answer any of the questions about Victor's death. What I could do was treat each day with my students like it was the only day we had. Not a dress rehearsal. Opening day. And honor his motto: "Aim High."

Always.

CHAPTER FIVE

ADVICE FROM A CATERPILLAR

I have often wondered about two things. First, why high school kids almost invariably hate the books they are assigned to read by their English teachers, and second, why English teachers almost invariably hate the books students read in their spare time. Something seems very wrong with such a situation. There is a bridge out here, and the ferry service is uncertain at best.
—Stephen King

*"You!" said the Caterpillar contemptuously. "Who are you?" Which brought them back again to the beginning of the conversation. Alice felt a little irritated at the Caterpillar's making such very short remarks, and she drew herself up and said, very gravely, "I think you ought to tell me who you are, first."
"Why?" said the Caterpillar.*
—Chapter Five,
Alice's Adventures in Wonderland

WHY NOT?

The wind-up timer sat on the kitchen counter. It wasn't for cooking. It was to limit my guilty conscience about "playing" with my children. They didn't count story time, play dough, neighborhood walks, Lego's, sandbox time, swings, or trips to the park. We did all that. Playing meant down on the floor, with their toys, in worlds they created. The rules were a mystery to me. There was a lot of building and tearing down, a fair amount of magic, good people and bad people, and talking animals. I spent a lot of time asking "Why is the raccoon mad at Cookie Monster?" or "Why are the Star Wars figures fighting GI Joe?"

"Why not?" they would say, followed by very detailed explanations. At the end of every playtime I thanked both my children and the toys, saying "See you tomorrow." I wasn't leaving the house. I was leaving the toy world. Though it wasn't how I remembered childhood play—paper dolls, pretending my bicycle was a horse, and never with Mother—I liked seeing them engaged, eager to begin, the director of the tales they wove.

In desperation I hit upon "one hour per day per child for toy-time" as a feeble attempt to maintain my sanity. I loved them but even love needs space. Maybe love especially needs space.

Most of the toys ended up, like toys always do, banished to storage, thrown out, or given away. But not all of them. Later, in the school where I got a job, I asked a Christian Brother if he could build shelves along the back wall. I took a few toys and tucked them among the workbooks and papers I stacked there. The teenagers asked, "Why are those games here?" My standard reply, "Why not?"

I taught a unit called "Fashioning the Hero." Part of the evaluation was a timed oral response to this prompt:

The Book of Job is often considered the greatest monument of Wisdom Literature in the Old Testament. Tennyson called it "the greatest poem of ancient and modern times." Carlyle declared, "There is nothing written, I think, in the Bible or out of it, of equal literary merit."

Is Job a hero? Thirty seconds exactly.

I used my old kitchen timer. A rubber Yoda sat nearby. They talked to him.

The test was near Halloween. One year after the exam the students presented me with a large black and purple sign. Scrawled across it were messages, strange symbols, lots of exclamation marks.

Yo, Koch, You're evil. Very, very evil! Cruel, unjust, insane. I love it. This class is a $5,000 freak show, to which I gladly pay admission. —Steve

Doc. I promise to turn in the rest of my test before I turn 21. You asked us at the beginning if we knew what human achievement could be defined as. I think I have a better idea now. —Shana

This was fun. You thank us. You care. I feel like a kid again. —Kat

In 2010, Pixar completed its 15-year Toy Story franchise. The New York Times described it as "a sweet, touching, humane adventure about a bunch of plastic toys and the child who owned them." It was more. It was a long meditation on loss, impermanence, and love. Many of my students are parents themselves now. I imagine them taking their offspring to see Woody, Buzz, and Andy—their children wondering, who is the hero?

Their parents can answer the question in thirty seconds. It's the person with a child-light inside, a faith that defies logic, and a heart big enough for the past and the future.

It's them.

In a minute or two the Caterpillar took the hookah out of its mouth, and yawned once or twice, and shook itself. Then it got down off the mushroom, and crawled away into the grass, merely remarking, as it went, "One side will make you grow taller, and the other side will make you grow shorter."
"One side of what? The other side of what?" thought Alice to herself.
"Of the mushroom," said the Caterpillar, just as if she had asked it aloud; and in another moment it was out of sight.
—Chapter Five
Alice's Adventures in Wonderland

The Radio Dial

*C*lassroom teachers are impatient with theories—at least theories about teaching. It is easy to understand. They're doing it. They don't have time for abstract ideas. They need practical solutions. For several years I taught university classes in summer and at night, high school during the traditional school year. Looking over the long, dry reading list for a Learning Theory graduate class I hadn't taught before, I sighed. It's reputation among students—inconsequential, irrelevant, irritating. It was required for their degree, which made them even grumpier. I needed a new approach. Forget the lecture on the origin of knowledge. What to do?

Reverse engineering. Today it is applied to technology. In August 2012, web news site Network World's lead story reported, "Pirated Mobile Android and Apple Apps Getting Hacked, Cracked, and Smacked." Fully 92 percent of the top hundred apps had been hacked in various ways. Between hacking, reverse engineering, and copying, mostly by China, the cost in lost revenue is estimated at $20 billion a year. Big problem.

But reverse engineering can make things better. In the Industrial

Age it meant taking something apart to see how it worked in order to enhance it. To look at structure, function, operation. I decided to structure the theory class around their classrooms—a project of deconstruction, analysis, evaluation of everything from style to content—by them. Based on the theorists we discussed, how could they explain their successes and failures? What needed change? Why did some things work, while others crashed?

I began with two questions for the back of their large yellow course-registration cards: One, write something you have learned to do. Two, define learning.

We talked about their answers, then tried to organize them. What did they have in common? Were there gaps in the framework we created?

The room filled with laughter, listening, discussion. It wasn't a conventional start. But it was a start. Graduate students vary widely in age, in background, in experience. Seeing what they had in common reminded us we were in the same story. The human story. A story we all wanted to improve.

One term I saved their registration cards. They reported:

I HAVE LEARNED
- To tie a tie.
- To walk.
- To understand other people's perspectives.
- To ride a bicycle.
- To figure out the standard deviation for a set of scores.
- To drive a car.
- To set rock climbing protection.
- To find the small things that make me happy.
- To draw a camel.
- To play music.
- To accept help from others.
- To have a positive outlook on life.

- To print like this.
- To climb back up again.

The term flew by. On final exam night I returned the yellow cards.
The directions: Based on your work this term, respond:

"Nature is like a radio band with infinite stations; the reality you are now experiencing is only one station on the band, completely convincing as long as you stay tuned to it, but masking the other choices that lie on either side."—Deepak Chopra.

Read your early definition of learning. What would you say now? Incorporate in your answer both the radio metaphor and your original definition.

The first line of your essay: "Classrooms hold the residue of theories once widely embraced but now supplanted. Using the radio metaphor, the culture was once tuned to otherworldly pursuits about what is worth knowing, followed by an earth-centered view of reality, and more recently a man-centered perspective."

"Taking things apart doesn't guarantee you can put them together again the same way," a student observed as he read.

"Do you want to?" I said.

A good high school math teacher is a particular gift. In the boys' high school where I spent 15 years there was one man, competent in his content area, but a disaster managing students. Without the second the first doesn't matter. One spring I spent several days watching a student in my class fiddling with a small mirror.

I wondered what he was doing. I walked over to him during an activity session. "What's up?" he said.

"I was thinking the same thing."

"What's with the mirror?"

A red flush crept up his neck. He said, "I didn't think you'd notice."

"I noticed. So, what's up?"

Gesturing out the window he said, "Look. I can catch the sun and reflect it into the classroom in the next building. It's driving the teacher crazy." He beamed as though this was a big accomplishment.

I got the mirror. He got to apologize to the math teacher, the unfortunate recipient of the light show. Later, the teacher said, "I don't understand it. You teach some classes one way and some another. It's inconsistent. I teach everything the same way. I'm consistent. I don't see why I have problems."

I was sympathetic. All teachers struggle. Most of the time I felt every class was a game of pick-up sticks—one slip and the whole pile would collapse. We had the same conversation many times. He felt the problem was the students. That was true, but he was part the solution. I never convinced him.

My colleague knew a great deal about math. He knew less about how students learn. I kept a radio in my classroom. I wondered if I should explain why I had it. It was to remind me. The radio needed adjusting depending on the air pressure and time of day. Otherwise it drifted into static that drowned the signal. Just like teaching.

One of my favorite professors often said, "Reality is a collective hunch. Science is a way to define reality based on objectivity. It's allowed us to be among the worst adapted creatures and still survive. We began with simple tools, and ended with the invention of theories. The better the theories, the more adaptable we are."

Alice in Wonderland is a story of change and adaptation. After her conversation with the Caterpillar, she continues to search for that beautiful garden. She comes upon

...an open place with a house in it about four feet high. "Whoever lives there," thought Alice, "it'll never do to come upon them this size: why, I should frighten them out of their wits!" So she began

nibbling at the right-hand bit again, and did not venture to go near the house until she had brought herself down to nine inches high.

At the end of the graduate course a student gave me a small orange sign. "Cookie cutter solutions are great if you're a cookie."

That's true. But students aren't cookies and single instructional approaches rarely work. The Caterpillar wasn't Alice's only teacher. Theory wasn't mine. But it helped.

Sometimes, though, the radio was most powerful when it was turned off. As Emerson said, "I like the silent church before the service begins, better than any preaching."

I concocted a special assignment for my wayward student. "Write a paper on light refraction and its applications in architecture. Five pages. Due in five days. If it's not turned in on time it will become ten pages. Use the writing skills you obviously have mastered since you have time to do science experiments with mirrors in English class."

"I was just having fun," he whined. "You can't make me write an essay about THAT. I don't have time. I have practice."

I stared at him. Silent.

At last he snatched the directions and stormed out. He turned in a good paper. Early. It was the last I saw of mirrors, from him or anyone else.

Radio bands and spaces. A theory about behavior and consequences. Lights reflected across classrooms for adults and teenagers.

Deepak Chopra—physician and spiritual writer. B.F. Skinner—psychologist and author.

Thank you both.

"Repeat 'You are old, Father William,'" said the Caterpillar.
Alice folded her hands and began:
"You are old, Father William," the young man said
"And your hair has become very white;
And yet you incessantly stand on your head—
Do you think, at your age, it is right?"
"That is not said right," said the Caterpillar. "It is wrong from begin-
ning to end."
—Chapter Five,
Alice's Adventures in Wonderland

WHERE TO BEGIN?

Harper Lee's *To Kill a Mockingbird* is a great book. Winner of the Pulitzer Prize in 1960. Never out of print since. Named one of the top 50 books of all time and the best book of the 20th century by the American Library Association. In 2006 British librarians ranked it ahead of the Bible as one book every adult should read before they die. It was the first book I taught as a new teacher. Not successfully. Neither then nor for years after. Every year I tried a new method. Every year brought mediocre results. It was a mystery.

I tried lots of ways to create interest:

TKM opens with the narrator reminiscing about the year her brother broke his arm. That seemed a good place to connect with teenagers. It wasn't.

The book is set in a small, sleepy town. Most teenagers thought their towns were sleepy. They could relate. They didn't want to. Another small town wasn't interesting.

The narrator talks about her ancestors. I asked students about their relatives. Not much reaction.

I told them it was a prize-winning story. They didn't care.

I divided the story into sections. I began at the beginning, assigned study questions to help them through the rural Southern setting. You could almost hear them snoring.

I promised the plot got interesting about Chapter Eleven—only a hundred pages to get through. They didn't believe me.

I loved the story. I hated teaching it. It was required. I put it first every September to get it over with. Another bad idea.

Summer was winding down. I eyed the calendar with despair. Out of time to read the mysteries and crime fiction I relished but never made any high school reading list. With only a few days left I skipped to the end of the mass-market paperback detective story on my nightstand, then returned to the beginning to see how the plot unfolded. So that's how it worked, I thought to myself. I wondered.

In academic classes teachers tell students to read the ends of chapters first to check the study questions or summaries. I said the same thing to aspiring teachers at Saint Mary's College in a course I taught—"Teaching Reading in the Secondary School." The student teachers were preparing in history, biology, chemistry, even the various math levels—algebra, geometry, statistics, and calculus. Potential language arts teachers didn't take the course. Apparently novels were different. They may be different, but sophomore students aren't going to wade through a hundred pages if a book doesn't catch them early on. No one is. Not even for a required book. A famous book.

To Kill a Mockingbird is at least two stories—a story about growing up and a story about courage. It is also a mystery. And a story about justice. And a story about race. All those ideas come together in the end. Why not start there?

On the first day of the *TKM* unit I looked out over the restless class.

"Let's start on page 207."

Voices rose around the room. Loud voices. "Whoa, Mrs. K! We

haven't even read page one."

Softer undercurrents. "She's scary. I told you."

"*TKM* is about lots of things. We'll find some together. Some you'll discover on your own. You won't agree on what the book is about. You don't have to. What you end up thinking about the book belongs to you. Your job will be to defend it."

I went on. "Atticus Finch is a hero in this story. He's not the only one. His closing speech to the jury in this tiny Southern Depression-era town still matters today. Please read along."

I closed the book and began to recite the summation speech Gregory Peck immortalized in the film:

"Thomas Jefferson once said that all men are created equal. There is a tendency in this year of grace, 1935, for certain people to use this phrase out of context, to satisfy all conditions. The most ridiculous example I can think of is that the people who run public education promote the stupid and idle along with the industrious—because all men are created equal, educators will gravely tell you, the children left behind suffer terrible feelings of inferiority. We all know men are not created equal in the sense some people would have us believe—some people are smarter than others, some people have more opportunity because they are born with it, some men make more money than others, some ladies make better cakes than others, some people are born gifted beyond the normal scope of most men. But there is one way...."

I finished with the powerful argument for the rule of law Harper Lee has Atticus argue to the jury at the conclusion of the trumped-up trial. My voice trailed off.

The class stared at me at though I had grown another head. "How did you do that without reading?"

"I memorized it," I said. "And so will you. Before the unit is finished every one of you will be able to recite this. It is worth as many points as an essay. You can do it in front of the class or by yourself at lunch or after school. No exceptions."

"I have never memorized anything for English," a boy frowned. "We're supposed to write and talk about ideas." He added for emphasis, "My father is a teacher in the City."

"Well, you're not in the City, you're here. And you'll do your share of writing. Don't worry. Think of it like brain calisthenics. Now let's talk about the story."

We started at the end. Went back to the beginning. Figured out how the plot worked, what it might mean. We talked about courage, compassion, feeling bullied, feeling left out. Winning and losing. Going along with the group. Standing alone. Through it all, people would pop up daily and say, "I'm ready to do the speech."

The powerful words were like a ribbon weaving around the package that became To Kill a Mockingbird. It was no longer a chore to teach or a chore to read. Memorizing has been out of fashion for decades. "It is a luxury we can no longer afford," says the former Director of Curriculum for the New York City Public Schools, Anita Dore. It's not a luxury. It's our heritage.

Generations of students grew up reciting Longfellow's "Listen my children and you shall hear / Of the midnight ride of Paul Revere…" I did. We practiced while we jumped rope. Most of us can still say it from memory. It's a connection to another time. To the children we were. To the dreams we shared. To the people the poem honored.

As I watched my students recite the stirring summation I imagined them as defenders of our best values when they became adults. Most are. It's why people teach.

The final exam was a single T.S. Eliot quote: "'What we call the beginning is often the end / And to make an end is to make a beginning. The end is where we start from.' Apply this to TKM. Does the book still matter?"

After the test the JV quarterback stopped at the door.

"That's the first long book I've ever read," he said. "I memorized another part too. Would you like to hear it?"

"Go for it."

Standing in the doorway he looked out toward the grassy quad. "It's when you know you're licked before you begin but you begin anyway and you see it through no matter what. You rarely win, but sometimes you do."

"Nice job."

"You know," he said. "About the test. Of course those ideas still matter. That was easy."

"Make sure you don't forget," I said. "It will be harder than you think."

Nodding, he hoisted his backpack and took off down the corridor.

Even a great book won't teach itself. It was the end of the unit. We'd be starting a new book. At the same time students were adding chapters to their own stories. Often they wove their reading and their lives together.

They took Atticus's speech with them. It's what Harper Lee intended.

So did I.

Part Three

CREATE

WHAT DO YOU NEED TO KNOW?

If the students don't have the basics, and if there is no one else to provide them, and if they need them before they can learn the advanced material, you have 3 choices: (1) plow into the advanced material, wasting both your time and theirs; (2) teach them the basics; (3) find another way for them to learn the basics—then teach the advanced material.
—Robert F. Mager

CHAPTER SIX

PIG AND PEPPER

The poet, as everyone knows, must strike his individual note some time between the ages of fifteen and twenty-five. He may hold it a long time, or a short time, but it is then that he must strike it or never. School and college have been conducted with the almost express purpose of keeping him busy with something else till the danger of his ever creating anything is past.
—Robert Frost

"If everybody minded their own business," the Duchess said, in a hoarse growl, "the world would go round a deal faster than it does."
"Which would not be an advantage," said Alice, who felt very glad to get an opportunity to showing off a little of her knowledge. "You see the earth takes twenty-four hours to turn round on its axis—"
"Talking of axes," said the Duchess, "chop off her head!"
—Chapter Six,
Alice's Adventures in Wonderland

UNEXPECTED DESTINATION

On a warm May afternoon in 1982 I stood at the podium, looking across the polished pews of the St. Mary's College Church, waiting for the graduate commencement program to begin. I spotted my mother. This speech was for her. She missed my high school graduation address 18 years before. I

89

stayed behind in San Diego while my Navy family moved to Washington, D. C. There wasn't enough money for both parents to fly back to California for graduation. My father came.

No one remembers valedictory speeches. She remembered this one. So did I.

I concluded:

> *Learning to read is one of the truly remarkable aspects of human behavior. Learning to read effectively in a variety of contexts and for a variety of purposes is even more remarkable. It is a long way, after all, from basal readers to the 472-word sentence in the third chapter of the Book of Luke. Helping students toward true literacy is a goal all of us in education share. In "The American Scholar" Ralph Waldo Emerson said, "Man is not a farmer, or a professor, or an engineer, but he is all. Man is priest, and scholar, and statesman, and producer, and soldier." I would add man is also a learner. I learned that from my mother.*

With only a high school diploma from a small Colorado town, she navigated the wide Navy world with common sense and a ferocious work ethic. I had figured that my new certificates and degree, together with my family upbringing, would make it easy to find a teaching job now that we were in California again. I figured wrong. Three unwelcome problems popped up. Budgets. Bridges. Biases.

I received my reading specialist license the month before the state legislature, in a cost-saving move, eliminated funding for all reading specialists. Through the years they have been reinstated and eliminated with as little logic as Alice found in Wonderland.

In spite of the funding cut, I applied to the sprawling Mount Diablo Unified School District in which I lived. The third-largest district in the state, it covers 150 square miles and serves 36,000 students on 56 campuses with a budget approaching $270 million.

I thought they might have more resource flexibility. "I am very sorry," said the clerk. In truth she didn't look sorry. She looked bored. "We're firing the reading specialists."

"What do you suggest?" I said.

The personnel department was noisy. Over the din of ringing telephones, clerks slamming file drawers, clicking keyboards, and the disconcerting drone of fluorescent lights she said, "Wait. Come back in a year or two. We'll probably get funding by then."

I felt like Alice talking to the footman at the Duchess's house as he tried to deliver an invitation to play croquet with the Queen.

> *"There's no use knocking," said the Footman, "because they're making such a noise inside, no one could possibly hear you." And certainly there was a most extraordinary noise going on within—a constant howling and sneezing, and every now and then a great crash, as if a dish or kettle had been broken to pieces. "How am I to get in?" asked Alice, in a louder tone. "Are you to get in at all?" said the Footman. "That's the first question, you know."*

Small towns or big cities. Lifestyle questions. Opportunity costs. Hours of discussion resulted in our Bay Area relocation from the Willamette Valley after ten years in the Northwest. An interesting challenge for my husband. More choices for me. That was the idea. The first part came true. He was energized by the chance to work for the country's largest public utility on issues that allowed him to bring theory and practice together. The one drawback—a daily commute back and forth across the Bay Bridge.

In Oregon, if I thought of bridges at all, it was to photograph the 20 or so quaint covered wooden structures dotting the countryside up and down the valley. In Eugene there was one bridge—the Ferry Street crossing. A modest 800 feet long, it was the shortest route over the Willamette River between the University of Oregon campus and

Autzen Stadium.

San Francisco was another story. Ten bridges sprinkle across eleven Bay Area counties. The most famous, the majestic Golden Gate connecting the city and Marin, celebrated its 75th anniversary on May 29, 2012. Of greater interest to me was the sturdy workhorse Oakland/San Francisco Bay Bridge. Four and a half miles long, its double-decker design has linked the East Bay to the city since 1936. Most days Jim left by 6 a.m. He walked to a busy intersection a mile away to catch a carpool for the 30-mile trip across town, through the Oakland hills and over the bridge. At the end of the day the process reversed. That meant I needed a job close to home. Geography limited my choices—not my desire.

One morning the summer after our move I drove past Carondelet, a Catholic girls' school 15 minutes from the house. I knew parochial schools still didn't require state credentials so I was sure having them would be an asset. They weren't. I decided to apply.

Today, people apply for jobs online. Everything is there…what positions are available, what qualifications are needed, what paperwork is required. Then, I went home, changed my clothes, gathered my resume, and returned the same afternoon.

Carondelet is across a narrow street from De La Salle, a boys' school run by the French Christian Brothers. Someone driving past the beautiful campuses might mistake them for a single school. Despite the similarities—imposing red brick buildings, chapels, acres of athletic fields, swimming pools, and parking lots filled with late-model cars—they operate as independent institutions. Different religious orders. Different genders. Different cultures.

The girls' school was the logical choice. If for no other reason than that I was a woman. And I had worked with the Holy Names community. Although the Sisters of Saint Joseph run Carondelet, I was confident the experience would help. I pulled open the sparkly glass entry door and approached the front desk.

"I'd like an application for a teaching position," I said with my best smile in place.

The receptionist looked up. She didn't smile back. "We have no positions available. We aren't taking applications now."

"I see," I said. "In that case, could I make an appointment for an informational interview?"

"Are you Catholic?"

I'd heard that question before. I was ready. "No. I'm not but—"

Before I could explain the woman interrupted: "We are interested in practicing Catholics. This IS a Catholic school."

Her mouth clamped shut in a straight, thin line. I was dismissed.

Back in the parking lot, I fumed. Frustrated. Frazzled. Fatigued. I had been planning my teaching return for a decade. The last three years I navigated graduate school in two states and a family move. I gazed across to the boys' school. "Why not there? Nothing ventured, nothing gained," I muttered.

I crossed the narrow street and wide parking lot, ending up in a narrow single-story building between the bookstore and the media center. A man and woman leaned against the counter.

"Excuse me," I said. "Can you tell me where to get a teaching application?"

They smiled. At least they are friendlier, I thought. They should be. These are Christian schools…not the DMV.

"What do you teach?" the woman said.

"English. Writing. Journalism. Reading. Study skills."

The man and woman exchanged glances.

"Can you teach sophomores?" he said.

"Yes, I can."

They introduced themselves…the Director of Studies and the English Department Chair.

"I have applications in my office," the woman said. "Come with me."

By the end of the month I had a job. No one asked if I was Catholic. Many asked if I understood the mission of Catholic schools. Most of the interview process was about content area requirements. How do you teach sophomores anyway?

This time I had answers. Twelve years removed from my first job, many things had changed. I was older. I had experienced more. Learned more. And I had become a parent of two boys.

Today there is a smartphone app called "Drift." The developers feel we have become a world where no one will ever be lost again. Turn-by-turn directions take us anywhere we want. Their idea is that a life without some unexpected detours is not nearly as satisfying as one with a few places we didn't expect to go on the way to destinations we program into the phone. I didn't have a smartphone in 1982. I did have two key people standing in the lobby of a school where I had no intention to apply that hot July afternoon.

Was it a coincidence?

Jean Baptiste De La Salle, founder of the Christian Brothers, was elevated to sainthood in 1900. He is the patron saint of teachers. For Christian Brothers education is practical, comprehensive, and available to everyone—not simply the wealthy. The Jesuits educated James Joyce, perhaps the greatest English author of all time. When his father fell into financial run and moved the family of ten to Dublin, the Christian Brothers educated the younger children.

The aristocrat De La Salle faced enormous budget problems, social barriers, political biases, in his quest to extend education. He succeeded. Today there are LaSallian schools in 85 countries. I am convinced his spirit was in the parking lot that summer day. Watching. Encouraging.

De La Salle was inclusive. The most powerful religious leaders always are. They invite everyone. I think he invited me because I believed in young people. They weren't a barrier to be beaten down or molded into some stifling social hierarchy.

They were the best kind of bridge. The one to tomorrow.

"What sort of people live about here?" Alice asked.
"In that direction," the Cat said, waving its right paw round, "lives a
Hatter: and in that direction," waving the other paw, "lives a March
Hare. Visit either you like: they're both mad."
"But I don't want to go among mad people," Alice remarked.
"Oh, you can't help that," said the Cat: "we're all mad here. I'm mad.
You're mad."
"How do you know I'm mad?" said Alice.
"You must be," said the Cat, "or you wouldn't have come here."
—Chapter Six,
Alice's Adventures in Wonderland

Who's Here?

*J*onathan Ive may never lead Apple Computer, but he might be its most important employee. For 14 years, as Apple's "star designer," he has worked to bring the company's iPod, iPhone, and iPad to market. His first hit was the original iMac computer, which made Apple "cool" again after Steve Jobs returned in 1997. Ive spent long hours in a candy factory "to get inspiration for the colors that told the world this wasn't 'just a machine for work.'" He labored for months on the stand for the desktop iMac "in pursuit of the sort of organic perfection found in sunflower stalks." Not accepting surface answers is a hallmark of his designs.

Faculty orientation meetings. Two long days that deflated my energy like air escaping a balloon. A parade of speakers cajoled, bellowed, lectured, explained our responsibilities: How to take attendance, when to dismiss students for breaks in the long 90-minute periods, what to do about eating in class, tobacco chewing, athletic early release procedures, how to reserve the library, where to sign up for prefecting supervision for the cafeteria, the parking lot, the back fields, the inner quad. For dances. Games. Assemblies. There was little mention of students. I wondered.

At breakout department meetings the teachers listened as the chair tried to engage us in curricular discussions. Should we keep electives or return to an anthology approach? How much homework? What kind of grading system? Is extra credit fair? The discussions were earnest and endless. Most of them have gone on unresolved for decades in most schools.

Several weeks earlier I met the department co-chair for a campus tour. I asked about the narrow doors with small overhead lights on the second floor breezeway.

"Those? They used to be confessionals. Now they are janitor closets," he said. Not the kind of Catholic schools the parents attended, I thought to myself. Is that a problem? I wondered.

Descending the cement stairs to ground level, he unlocked the second door on the right. Room 202. My future classroom.

Pulling open the heavy door, I stepped inside. Teachers are lucky to have a designated room of their own. I did a little jig across the threshold—then stopped short. Outdated pull-down maps hung on the back wall. Others were propped next to a dented file cabinet like giant pick up sticks. A television was mounted in one corner on a swivel arm. Torn and droopy beige vinyl drapes crammed behind it on a long rod that stretched along the wall of windows overlooking a parking lot.

Bulletin boards were covered with out-of-date announcements, faded flyers, the bell schedule, and fire escape directions. A tall storage cabinet in the back right corner was filled with old workbooks, mismatched construction paper, and trash. The wall clock near the door didn't work. I half expected to see Dickens' Miss Havisham lurking in the corner. In his *Great Expectations*, she stopped all the clocks in her dusty old mansion at 20 minutes to nine—the moment she learned her lover jilted her on their wedding day. Room 202 looked like it could easily slip into that discarded world. The classroom was neglected, as though the previous occupant had left in a rush, not bothering to leave it an inviting space, or even a clean one. I wondered.

Back in the office, the chairman handed me a tall stack of paperbacks for the courses I was assigned.

"You'd be smart to read them before the year starts," he said. "Do you have any questions?"

"What about the students? What are they like? What can I expect?"

He shrugged. "Handling 30 or so teenage boys at a time is tough. They're not especially interested in English. I'm sure you understand that."

"Why do parents send their kids here?" I pressed.

"Some for the sports. Some for the discipline. Some for religious education. Some for academics." He chuckled.

His answers were different from what I heard when I was hired. I got an idea.

"Do you have a yearbook I could borrow?"

Balancing the tower of paperbacks on top of the large book he loaned me, I headed home.

Poring over its contents, I found what I needed. Who knows best about a school? Custodians, cafeteria workers, clerical staff. People who interact with the students outside the confines of the classroom. Every day I went to campus for several hours. I cleaned. I wandered around. I found the cafeteria manager. Her stories of the lunchroom—jostling and cutting in line, trash, chaotic noisy eating and occasional food fights—made me think one of two things was occurring: either classes were so strict students were letting off steam, or the reverse. Classes were so loose the behavior seemed normal. It was a little of both.

The custodial shed stood near a tall eucalyptus tree at the back edge of campus. The plant supervisor had his own tales of broken desks and lockers, graffiti, and more trash. "We have so many seagulls foraging in the quad after lunch and break it's hard to believe we're 35 miles from the ocean," he said.

The attendance clerk had stories too. Besides attendance she was running an informal "support group." It was a haven for boys out of class for all manner of reasons every day…thrown out, walked out of their own accord, or who didn't get there in the first place. She was providing a safety valve for tired, troubled teens—off the radar.

Armed with so much confusing information, I faced 150 high school students for the first time in over a decade in September 1982. The Dean caught up with me on my way to class. "Remember," he said. "Don't smile until Thanksgiving." It was advice I heard before. I never understood it. If we don't like what we're doing why would anyone else enjoy it?

The first day at Saint Monica's ten years earlier, I stood behind the desk as students entered, fixated on my lesson plan, even though I knew it inside out. This time I stood at the door every period, greeting each boy, smiling, looking straight at them. It was like being a flight attendant at an aircraft entry hatch. Tall or short, chubby or gangly, faces acne-covered, clear skinned, or faintly stubbled. Mohawk haircuts or shaggy. Trench coats, athletic jerseys, tee shirts announcing allegiance to rock groups I didn't know: "The Police." "Def Leppard." "Aerosmith." Teenagers—who could read, who couldn't, who wouldn't. Every personality type: Eddie-Haskell smarmy, the shy, the loud, the sullen, the defiant, the bored, the clueless, the bullies, the drug dealers, the scholars, the athletes, the gamers. Students lugging backpacks, students carrying nothing. An astonishing array of boys shuffled into Room 202 day after day.

In an instant I stopped wondering about the conflicting, confusing information that bombarded me before school started. I knew. Parents send their children to Catholic schools for all the reasons my Department chair pointed out—athletic hopes, religious influences, academic aspirations for the gifted and the struggling—but they also send them hoping someone will actually SEE their children, and care for them. It was what I wanted as a parent myself. It was the place to begin: Care first. Curriculum second.

Jonathan Ive has become fabulously wealthy at Apple by attending to every design detail. According to a 2012 *The Week* magazine article, he still gets "an incredible thrill" from seeing someone wearing Apple's trademark white ear buds. "But I'm constantly haunted by thoughts of, 'Is good enough? Is there any way we could have made it better?'"

I didn't spend my career thinking about computer stands and ear-bud designs, but I admire the patience and discovery process that created objects we take for granted. It is the same patience that helps teachers see beyond what might look like a disinterested teenager, hear beyond what their music blares, uncover what we miss when we accept other people's explanations for behavior we don't understand.

Teachers never become wealthy. They do inherit a readymade family of students of every age to love, to worry over, to care about. Like our own children, students grow up. In leaving they often left notes behind. Some looked like these:

Mrs. Koch (aka Mom): You've helped me grow in my faith and you've helped me get through some rough times. I hope you never lose your desire to share your love with those who need it.—Lynne (a journalist)

Mrs. Koch: I came into this class very unsure about both myself and my English abilities. I am now leaving with more confidence in myself than I ever dreamed of having. —Shannon (a teacher)

Mrs. Koch: I couldn't have done it without the hugs and encouragement. I'm finally starting to think non-linearly. Thanks for having patience with us—I know my writ-

*ing has improved. But I still have calculus to rot my mind!
Love, Chris (a doctor)*

*Alice wanted to play croquet with the Queen. "I should like it
very much," she said, "but I haven't been invited yet."
"You'll see me there," said the Cat, and vanished.
Alice was not much surprised at this, she was getting so well used
to queer things happening. While she was still looking at the
place where it had been, it suddenly appeared again. "I wish you
wouldn't keep appearing and vanishing so suddenly; you make
one quite giddy!"
"All right," said the Cat; and this time it vanished quite slowly
beginning with the end of the tail, and ending with the grin,
which remained some time after the rest of it had gone.*

My students have vanished. All that remains is the memory of
their smiles.

It's enough.

She had not gone much farther before she came in sight of the house of the March Hare: she thought it must be the right house, because the chimneys were shaped like ears and the roof was thatched with fur. It was so large a house, that she did not like to go near till she had nibbled some more of the left-hand bit of mushroom, and raised herself to about two feet high...
—Chapter Six,
Alice's Adventures in Wonderland

Boxes, Banners, and Batwings

*H*ome decorating is big business. A quick Yahoo search shows 448,000,000 online possibilities. Feng shui to shabby chic, contemporary to retro, country to eclectic—something for everyone. They all focus on transformation from tired or broken or unpleasant to a better reflection of the owner's interests and desires. In October 2012 *Country Living* magazine featured two men who restored an antebellum home in Madison, Georgia. The 1818 building laid claim to being the oldest brick structure in town. The owners, interior designer Jimmy Stanton and his partner Patrick Greco, wanted a retreat from their hectic Atlanta lives. The article details the renovation that "ignored the usual heavy period style in favor of their own eclectic approach."

After cleaning the empty rectangular room where I'd be spending the next 180 days, one word came to mind—sterile. It looked like every other room stretching along the corridor—beige, bland, boring. How could I create a retreat for my students and me? Then I remembered.

Her name was Edna Bruce. She was my high school senior Civics teacher 25 years before. Barely five feet tall, with white hair and a round wrinkled face, she looked deceptively like the fairy godmother in "Cinderella." She was the brain behind the elaborate Nominating Convention the high school held every year before student body elections. Operated like the national conventions, every history class elected representatives to form delegations. Candidates registered, gathered signatures on petitions, and gave speeches during campaign week prior to the election itself. The school was transformed into a festival of light, posters, sounds, and intense lobbying for one or another candidate. It was democracy in action. Mrs. Bruce was the driving force.

She was ferocious. One of her senior classes built her an enormous blue wooden dragon. It filled her entire back classroom wall from the ceiling to the bottom of the blackboard. She terrified students. They called her "the dragon lady." Every spring a nervous parade of juniors flooded the office with creative excuses for avoiding her. She taught the only subject everyone had to pass to graduate. The stakes were high. When I got my schedule there it was—"CIVICS—Mrs. Bruce." My heart sank. In the end it turned out to be my best and favorite high school class.

Even the rowdiest boys transformed under her laser gaze. She created an environment where we all mattered. She didn't let people raise their hands. She called on everyone. It was refreshing to not have to listen to the same handful of people who dominated most class discussions. When she retired the school left the dragon up in her classroom, but the magic was gone. Whenever I consider, even for a moment, not voting, I see Mrs. Bruce and banish the thought. Students often told me Civics and government were boring. What a shame. We thought it was the most exciting class in school.

I bought three stuffed winged dragons for the unappealing classroom. Green, purple, and mauve. I named them Odysseus, Penelope, and Telemachus for characters in Homer's *Odyssey*. I told the students dragons represented imagination and the determination it would take to get out of the boxes we were in—the classroom itself and the mental barriers we erect that interfere with thinking.

Later Yoda, who sat on the overhead projector, joined the dragons. I sat them on students' desks for all kinds of reasons: if someone looked down, or unprepared, or especially happy. All of them had harrowing adventures. Students kidnapped them. Ransom notes demanded everything from project extensions to food in class. Yoda lost his hair. Meanwhile, Odysseus disappeared for an entire year until a sheepish cross-country runner found him in the bottom of his gym bag.

Some of my colleagues found the whole process irritating. "Stuffed animals have no place in a high school," one grumbled.

"Dragons have nothing to do with the curriculum," said another.

"They're not stuffed dragons," I said. "They're imaginations at work. Remember Einstein? 'Imagination is more important than knowledge.'" They weren't convinced.

Meanwhile, students began bringing pennants from colleges they visited to join my own UCLA banner. Over time more than a hundred crammed the room's perimeter—colorful reminders of the students who lived in the box before and the dreams they had. Large universities. Small colleges. Ivy League. Big Ten. Party schools. Serious ones. Urban campuses. Mountain retreats. Beach settings. Catholic. Public. Private. Liberal arts. Technical schools. Military academies. Seminaries. There are over 3500 colleges and universities in the United States. They chose well and widely.

I had bought posters at a school supply shop—the kind of inspirational sayings one sees in athletic apparel stores. "Go the distance!" "Power on!" After my own children's Back to School night I realized my students needed to see their work in the classroom—not someone else's. I yanked the posters down. The room became a forest of projects, signs, mobiles hanging from the ceiling, models snaking around the floor, as creative teenagers showed they understood what they were studying in every possible format.

Some made movies. Some built elaborate Lego projects. Bumper stickers covered the file cabinets. DANGER—POISON with a skull and crossbones hung on the television. They wrote every day. Sometimes a sentence. Sometimes a page. Sometimes on lined paper. Sometimes on blank sheets. Sometimes in symbols. Sometimes in algebraic formulas. Sometimes a paragraph—but only if they could convince me the sentences were actually related to one another.

The box. First empty. Then filled with images of past and present. The room looked like what it was—a busy energetic place.

Students not enrolled wandered in and out. Parents visited. One wrote:

> *Madeline and I really enjoyed our tour of the box yesterday, and we couldn't be happier with the progress Kevin has made as a confident, more creative, and interested student as a result of this experience. He seems to be really trying to think his way through the material and express his ideas as opposed to just replaying data like a Walkman. I couldn't help but notice among your many trophies from universities there was a CORNELL pennant. No self respecting COLGATE graduate could let that go unanswered, so I felt it necessary to provide you with this well-worn pennant from my collection. – Tom*

Interior designer Stanton and his partner found a shabby antebellum mansion and renovated it to reflect their appreciation for its history and an enthusiasm for the present. I wanted the same for my classroom, with one addition—a path to the future.

I didn't need to bring it, or assign it, or hang it up, or build it. Teachers can help interpret the past and present. Students find the future on their own.

CHAPTER SEVEN

A Mad Tea Party

That men do not learn very much from the lessons of history is the most important of all the lessons that history has to teach.
—Aldous Huxley

There was a table set out under a tree in front of the house, and the March Hare and the Hatter were having tea at it: a dormouse was sitting between them, fast asleep, and the other two were using it as a cushion, resting their elbows on it, and talking over its head. The table was a large one, but the three were all crowded together at one corner of it. "No room! No room!" they cried out when they saw Alice coming.
"There's plenty of room!" said Alice indignantly, and she sat down in a large armchair at one end of the table.
—Chapter Seven
Alice's Adventures in Wonderland

Plenty of Room

Tracking. It's an old story. About class. Color. Control. Sol Cohen describes the process in "The Industrial Education Movement, 1906-1917." Typical of the arguments is the one given by the Cleveland superintendent of schools in April 1910 issue of *Educational Review*:

"It is obvious that the educational needs of children in a district where the streets are well paved and clean, where the homes are spacious and surrounded by lawns and trees, where the language of the child's playfellows is pure, and where life in general is permeated with the spirit and ideals of America, it is obvious that the educational needs of such a child are radically different from those who live in a foreign and tenement section."

Desegregation after 1954 brought change in some community organizations—most notably Southern city councils. It didn't extend to schools. Tracking and ability grouping continue everywhere based on color, not competence. The situation in Selma, Alabama, is one example. Even in 1990 the tracked high school's upper-ability program had nearly all white students, and only three-percent Black students. Professor William Bernard at the University of Alabama calls tracking "great change and no change." Schools are unequal places.

The Christian Brothers didn't have many Honors classes. Instead, they offered a "comprehensive curriculum," which meant students could self-select based on their interests: from general math to calculus, from physical science to physics, from basic writing to creative writing to technical writing; from survey literature to specialized topics: California Writers, The Short Story, Books of Beasts, Classics of Horror. Across the street, the girl's school did offer Advanced Placement English. The unintended outcome: students felt the more serious English classes weren't available at De La Salle. It wasn't true, and it wasn't helpful.

"Why don't we offer an Advanced Placement class?" I asked the department chair.

"We have in the past," he said, "but the entire program is strong. We don't need to stratify that way."

While it is not unusual for private schools to adopt that stance, it was clear students were at a disadvantage in the escalating college entrance race where Honors and Advanced courses boosted grade-point averages. Distasteful as it may be, it is a fact of life. In the hierarchy of traditional curriculums Advanced Placement courses theoretically loom above even the Honors courses. Students earned extra grade-point calculations for AP work. Their appeal was not so much the coursework, but the edge it gave college applications.

"Can I submit an Advanced Placement English proposal?"

"Even it we approve it and the College Board accepts it," he said, "you'll need pre-requisites. What will they be?"

Most schools required a writing sample, a teacher recommendation, and a robust grade-point average. All normal. I had a different idea. With the support of the chair and over the objections of some faculty, we reinstated Advanced Placement English. The single pre-requisite was a two-sentence contract. It read: "I have read the course objectives and I understand them. I am willing to commit myself to meeting them in this academic year."

It was a pledge about perseverance. About pushing boundaries. About risking grade-point averages. About doing their best. The pre-requisite was motivation. Many years later the College Board announced AP classes should be open to any willing high schooler. Students should recognize, however, that dropping classes and wreaking havoc with their academic schedules is undesirable, so "unusual profiles" would benefit from counseling prior to enrolling. We knew that from the start.

I taught more than a few "unusual profiles" over the next dozen years. One boy spent most of his time in the imaginary world of Dungeons and Dragons. Another dressed entirely in black and prided himself on opening the storage closet in the back of the room with his lock-picking set. They were fun, fascinating, fearless.

More challenging were some of the conventionally qualified...the boy headed to the Ivy League whose primary activity was keeping his hoody over his head and belittling others, or the student-body president who slammed his hand through the window when he didn't finish a timed writing...missing the point about planning. Today he is a government bureaucrat.

In addition to AP I taught two sections of sophomores: one from the small Honors curriculum and one regular section. I was struck by how few differences there were between them. The most obvious: students in the Honors section felt they were "smarter." One year among the 60 teenagers in both sections Steve was the top student—and he was in the regular track. He was a soccer player. He hunched over his classwork, clutching a pencil, chewing on his lip, as he worked through study questions and activities. He was serious about the class and the classwork. It wasn't unusual to hear his cheerful yell, "Hey, Mrs. Koch," as he hurried by the door at the end of the day on his way to practice or to the weight room.

One day in the spring of his junior year he stuck his head in. "Are you busy?"

"Hi, Steve. Forget something?"

He shifted his backpack and brushed the hair out of his eyes. "I've been thinking about Advanced Placement," he said. "Do you think I could sign up?"

"Why?"

"I didn't take Honors before, but I know I can do it. Athletics are important, but with my size I won't be recruited. I want to be a lawyer."

I studied the lanky earnest teenager. He didn't have a conventional Honors profile. He did have the desire. Harder to measure. More important to consider.

"I'll look forward to seeing you next fall."

Charles Osgood is an American television and radio reporter. On CBS since 1971, he hosted a weekday radio program "The Osgood Files." In 1990 he was inducted into the National Association of Radio Broadcasters. Students today recognize him as the narrator of the 2008 film "Horton Hears a Who."

On the first day of Advanced Placement, I asked students to read an Osgood poem. I used the Quaker "read aloud" approach. Someone would volunteer, read a little and then stop. Someone else would pick up. It involves everyone who wants to be involved. It encourages sharing. It lets people hear different voices. At the top of the handout I wrote "The Gift of Reading."

There once was a pretty good student
Who sat in a pretty good class
And was taught by a pretty good teacher
Who always let pretty good pass.
He wasn't terrific at reading,
He wasn't a whiz-bang at math,
But for him, education was leading
Straight down a pretty good path.
He didn't find school too exciting,
But he wanted to do pretty well,
And he did have some trouble with writing
Since nobody taught him to spell.
. . .
The pretty good class that he sat in
Was part of a pretty good school,
And the student was not an exception:
On the contrary, he was the rule.
The pretty good student in fact was
Part of a pretty good mob.
And the first time he knew what he lacked was
When he looked for a pretty good job.
It was then, when he sought a position,
He discovered that life could be tough,
And he soon had a sneaky suspicion
Pretty good might not be good enough.
The pretty good town in our story

Was part of a pretty good state
Which had pretty good aspirations
And prayed for a pretty good fate.
There once was a pretty good nation
Pretty proud of the greatness it had,
Which learned much too late,
If you want to be great,
Pretty good is, in fact, pretty bad.

—*The Osgood File*, 1986, CBS, Inc.

"Think about this for a few minutes. Shut your eyes."

The rustling died down. I closed my eyes too. In the quiet I meditated on the days ahead. Wondering. Wishing. Worrying.

"One last thing before you decide if you're staying or going," I said.

On the overhead projector I slapped a transparency. Written in blue:

THIS COURSE HAS A POINT OF VIEW

1. There are no works here which can be read once and expected to stay read.
2. Learning to write is always about to begin.
3. The discussion questions don't work from preconceived point to point. They are meant as possible ways to begin thinking about endless matters.
4. Revision and rewriting are taken for granted.
5. If you'd like to leave, see the Director of Studies today.

In twelve years the Director processed two transfer requests.

Steve stayed. Before graduation he brought me an engraved stapler. Black with chrome trim, a tiny plaque perched on top. "To Mrs. Koch—Love, Steve." He attached a note: "To help you keep your students' revisions together next year. They'll be surprised how many there are. I was."

Today Steve is a successful attorney. He didn't have conventional prerequisites. It didn't matter. He made the class better. He's a reminder—tracks take people somewhere, but they can be arbitrary, inaccurate, alienating when they keep people stuck in classifications designed more to stratify than empower.

Chances. Choices. Challenging convention. Schools can do that. Some do.

Some isn't enough.

*"Have you guessed the riddle yet?" the Hatter said, turning to Alice
again.
"No, I give it up," Alice replied. "What's the answer?"
"I haven't the slightest idea," said the Hatter.
"Nor I," said the March Hare.
Alice sighed wearily. "I think you might do something better with
the time," she said, "than wasting it in asking riddles that have no
answers."*
—Chapter Seven
Alice's Adventures in Wonderland

Puzzles, Parables, and Prizes

In 1983 William Golding won the Nobel Prize in Literature
for, among other things, *Lord of the Flies*, his parable of
English schoolboys who are deposited for safekeeping on a coral
island while their elders wage nuclear war. Slowly they revert
to savagery. In a *Time* magazine article after the award he said,
"The theme is an attempt to trace the defects of society back to
the defects of human nature." Golding was publishing poetry
and working in regional theater when World War II began. He
joined the Royal Navy, witnessed the sinking of the Bismarck,
and took part in the Normandy invasion. From then on, for him,
the human race was inherently evil. I taught the novel the first
time the year he won the Nobel. People said it was easy to teach:
follow-the-dots symbolism, an author who says what the theme is,
and enough violence to appeal to teenage boys. I didn't think so.

The bell rang. Classroom sounds—conversations, scraping chairs,
thuds as backpacks hit the floor—died down. It's like the restless fidg-
eting in pews that stops as church services begin. Thirty 15-year-old
boys. It felt like being stuck on an island. The teaching challenge is
always the same: engage, energize, educate. They knew the basic story.

Most of them had seen the movie. My design idea was a variation on the conventional approach of having students simulate forming groups as if they were marooned.

"I'm going to be outside the room for 20 minutes," I said. "While I'm gone, figure out how you'd like to be organized the next three weeks for studying *Lord of the Flies*."

I filled in more specifics on a transparency: Who would you choose as leader? What would you need to do to survive? What kind of government would you devise? Who do you want with you? Leaving the projector on, I dragged a chair into the corridor and shut the door behind me. After 10 minutes or so the muffled sounds from inside grew louder. After 15 minutes the teacher next door stormed out. "What are you doing?" he snapped. "We can't hear over your noise."

My noise? It wasn't my noise. True to my word, I stepped back inside after 20 minutes. The desks were shoved into two facing heaps like a racetrack pileup. Two boys had taken the metal center pulls from the back file cabinet and were "sword fighting" to the cheers of most of the others. None of the questions on the overhead had been completed. The machine was unplugged and shoved under a long table. Three or four boys stood together away from the chaos, drawing superheroes on the blackboard.

Brandon looked at me. "This is gay. These guys are weak. I could write a better story myself."

Reining in 30 boys isn't easy unless you are a coach or a mother. I was both. I turned off the classroom lights, raised my voice in the same tone my own mother used and said, "OK, what's happening? Hush. Now."

Students milling around the wreck of the classroom stopped moving. Zorro and his partner separated. Silence descended like a lid slammed on a gurgling pot. "Golding is right," someone muttered.

"Put the desks back and sit down," I said in the tone every mother uses to make children feel guilty. Guilt is a wonderful thing.

The period was almost over. Their faces mirrored their thinking:

unsure, uneasy, uncomfortable.

"We know what Golding thinks about man," I said. "We know how you behaved this afternoon. What we don't know is why you behaved like you did. Or why the characters in *Flies* did either."

I passed out the unit project—the cover a collage of peculiar shapes overlaid in bold with the words CRACKING THE CODE. "You're more complicated than what we saw today." I went on. "*Lord of the Flies* doesn't explain all human behavior. It's a puzzle. Let's see what we find out beyond the obvious—about the book characters and about people you know. Your homework—one paragraph: Did you make things better or worse today?"

We started far from the book. We talked about Pogo's pronouncement, "We have met the enemy and he is us." We read excerpts from *Out of Weakness*, a book by Harvard professor Andrew Schmookler, who argued that because we deny our internal conflicts we engage in external aggression. The local paper reported the anniversary of Japan's decision to send kamikaze pilots to the Philippines to attack American ships as World War II ground on. Some of the students were Filipino. They knew Japanese felt they would become "living gods," living forever in a pantheon of nation-saving heroes at Tokyo's Yasukuni Shrine, through their sacrifices. We talked about honor. We read *Tarzan* and the *Jewels of Opar*.

I asked some of them to draw football plays on the board and explain—not the X's and O's but the lines and arrows crossing back and forth and around. I described the idea of "force fields" that push people one way or another.

I explained psychologist Lawrence Kohlberg's "Stages of Moral Development" concept. His work, adapted from Piaget, identifies six stages of moral reasoning from amorality to universal consciousness. Like Kohlberg, I used the "Heinz Dilemma" to illustrate the stages.

Heinz's wife was near death. Her only hope was an expensive drug which cost $20,000 to manufacture. The pharmacist would sell it for $200,000. Heinz could only raise $50,000. His offer was rejected. He said he would pay more later. The pharmacist still refused. Heinz considered stealing the drug. Would that be wrong?

Students argued. Defended their answers. They were close to ready for the book. Their project would create force fields to illustrate what pushed characters toward one problem resolution or another. They would analyze situations characters faced in terms of Kohlberg.

Finally, we analyzed the parable of the Good Samaritan in Luke 10:30–37. It is easy to see where the narrative stops and the theme starts—a directive of care and compassion in a world of thieves. Eight days passed before we plowed into the Golding text.

The students brought their "Cracking the Code" projects on exam day. I collected them. They waited for the exam papers. I fished out my directions from day one: "If you were marooned on an island." I put the transparency back on the overhead.

"I'll be back in 30 minutes," I said. "This is the exam."

Sitting outside, I didn't hear a sound. A half hour later I opened the door. The boys had organized the desks in small groups around a central collection of chairs. They had set up a government, picked a president, policemen, lookout people, planners, builders, and cooks. They made a chart on the board diagramming their choices based on a frank understanding of their classmates and a clever grasp of Kohlberg. They were more than survivors. They were shapers of a better world.

Golding was a controversial choice for the Nobel Prize. He is a master of simple despair. Most art contains elements of surprise. Young people, comfortable with puzzles, curious about behavior, recognized that Golding didn't capture all of what mankind is—Nobel laureate or not. They knew they weren't simple. Neither is the world.

That understanding is a better prize. More hopeful. More helpful. For all of us.

Once more she found herself in the long hall, and close to the little
glass table. "Now, I'll manage better this time," she said to herself,
and began by taking the little golden key, and unlocking the door
that led into the garden. Then she set to work nibbling at the mush-
room (she had kept a piece of it in her pocket) till she was about a
foot high: then she walked down the little passage: and then—she
found herself at last in the beautiful garden, among the bright
flower beds and the cool fountains.
—Chapter Seven,
Alice's Adventures in Wonderland

A Golden Key

*T*eachers are trained in formulaic approaches to lesson design. Most begin with variations on a lockstep process: Get their attention. State the objective. Pretest. Teach. Test. Move on.

At Saint Mary's College I taught a required secondary credential course for several years. At first I was excited to be part of the college faculty. Soon I realized we weren't doing any favors assigning one-month "design units" to prospective teachers. The units met the Commission on Teacher Credentialing requirements. Student-teachers presented detailed lessons in their content areas—30 days marching one after another like soldiers on a cross-country trek. There were elaborate Civil War reenactments, the evolution of bird beaks, the physics of volleyball shots. Every day laid out. Every strand of the state requirements covered. The college was happy. Its own accreditation depended on its students meeting scope requirements for licensing. Our courses reflected state mandates. Politics drove decisions about what to teach, when to teach it, sometimes even providing scripts for how to teach it.

One student, a serious young woman teaching English on an emergency credential, came to see me.

In a voice so soft I strained to hear she said, "The unit isn't working. You said it was good. It isn't. I am on Day 19 and almost no one is with me. Now what? We have to move on to the drama unit in two weeks."

"Where did you lose the class?" I asked. "Go backwards. Figure out what broke."

"How do I do that?" she said.

"Ask the kids."

"I don't have time to go back. They don't connect to the book."

"Have you taken ed theory courses?"

"No. I want the credential. I don't need theory. It's not practical."

"There's nothing more practical than a good theory," I snapped. "And that's not my idea. It's Kurt Lewin's." She stared. I caught myself. No point in taking out my frustrations on her. The teacher was on overload. Too many expectations. Not enough control over her own professional destiny. "Never mind," I sighed.

"Turn in the unit. It meets the course requirement. Let's put it aside and talk about where your class is. That's where you need to be too."

I stopped teaching the credential class. It satisfied the state. It failed the teachers. Worse, it failed their students. Years later I began teaching elective courses in another master's program. More freedom for me. More help for them. Who decides what is required, I wondered? We're like the Hatter's tea party. It's always six o'clock. "Yes, that's it," said the Hatter with a sigh: "it's always tea-time, and we've no time to wash the things between whiles." Teachers don't have time either. We need it.

Students are on a path along which growth is a natural condition. We don't need to focus solely on what they now find relevant. What we need to do is create and model experiences that connect to where they are now. Myles Horton, in his book *We Make the Road by Walking*, speaks of the thread that connects a person's past experience to new knowledge when he says, "If you do this thing right, carefully, and don't get beyond participants at any one step, you can move very fast to expand their experience very wide in a very short time. But you have to always remember, if you break that connection, it's no longer available to their experience, then they don't understand it, and it won't be useful to them."

This is the essence of relevance. Without it there is no way for a student to grab real, lasting meaning. Paulo Freire, speaking to Horton in his book, adds, "Starting from people's experiences, and not from our understanding of the world, does not mean that we don't want the people to come with us in order to go beyond us afterward."

The center of my teaching rested on Freire. In 1980 I read *Literacy and Revolution: The Pedagogy of Paulo Freire* by Robert Mackie. I discovered a blueprint that defined the rest of my career. Freire emphasized dialogue with respect. Not one person acting on another, but rather people working with one another. He argued too much education involved "banking"—making deposits in someone else's thinking. The alternative—two participants—which leads to transformation for both.

The Air Force Academy assigned freshmen an essay, "Applying Freire to Your Own Experience." After Victor Nigro's death it was among his papers. Victor wrote in part:

> *Teachers can teach through many methods. In the beginning they should use Freire's banking concept. This lets the instructor teach through lectures and exercises which are specifically followed by the students. Learning the alphabet or memorizing multiplication tables are good examples of the usefulness of the banking concept. This type of teaching establishes a foundation of knowledge.*
>
> *After students have learned the basics, teachers should use Freire's problem solving method. This causes the students to work on*

their own in a creative manner. The students have the freedom to solve a problem in any way possible, as long as they support their conclusions.

Victor went on to describe our Advanced Placement class versus another class taught with a banking method. The second teacher required starting specific sentences with specific words, specific sentence length, strict class behavior, singular focus on the nation-wide test. She explained her interpretation of the literature. Then students repeated what she said in their essays.

Victor concluded:

Freire believes problem solving makes the student "conscious" of himself and of the real world. If we don't reject banking people end up with "a fragmented view of reality, alienated, and domes-ticated." My class studied "Oedipus Rex" in an intensive week after the teacher taught us many techniques for approaching and interpreting the material. She let us interpret the readings the way we saw them. The other class spent a month. They wrote one essay in the teacher's style. The results were students who became unmotivated and confused. They got less accomplished. In the end the students felt unprepared for the test they had set out to prepare for. We didn't. We worked harder. We did different kinds of projects besides essays. We had fun. The test was never the focus of our class. The ideas were important. We passed anyway. Best of all, we were confident we had tools we could use in the future. There will always be new problems. We're ready.

Victor was right about Freire. Sometimes people need specific instruction. Sometimes they need answers. Sometimes they need more time. Sometimes they need less. Victor's class spent one week on *Oedipus*. Other years took longer. Once we spent two days. It was all the students needed. One year I stayed on Day 78 of my syllabus for a month. They weren't ready to move on.

Paulo Freire has many critics. Scholars don't like the religious overtones, his simplistic view of change, the difficulties of his dense language. Perhaps. What he does offer is a way to attack apathy and disinterest. A way to empower people by engaging them in a language of possibility. The possibility of dialogue as a way to name and understand the world through a different lens.

"You shouldn't talk," said the Hatter.
This piece of rudeness was more than Alice could bear: she got up
in great disgust, and walked off. The dormouse fell asleep instantly,
and neither of the others took the least notice of her going. "I'll
never go there again," she said, as she picked her way through the
wood. "It's the stupidest tea-party I ever was at in all my life!"
Chapter Seven
Alice's Adventures in Wonderland

CODA: A GOLDEN KEY

When Alice leaves the tea party and enters the garden at last, she has reached a new stage in her adventure. If the story were a classic five-act play this would be Act III—a climax. A place where she finally has confidence in her own understanding. Confidence to do something on her own. Confidence to defy convention.

I arrived in my own garden after many years in other people's stories. I was lucky to be in a school that gave its teachers room to experiment. A school where the motto was "Enter to learn. Leave to serve." It could have been the Chinese proverb, "To know and not to act is not to know." Catholic schools are more ragged than public schools because they are less constrained by state bureaucracy. But when they are good, they are very good. De La Salle was one of those schools. Far from perfect. But engaged in the business of transformation. For students. For families. For teachers. For communities.

As part of *The Canterbury Tales* students undertook a character analysis of any pilgrim they chose. Their work was detailed, text-based, and reflected Chaucer's era.

As was my custom, I wanted the work to be non-linear and include input beyond from "beyond the box"—in this case with nuns and priests they knew. The room filled with three-dimensional figures hanging everywhere. The most colorful were the religious travelers—the pardoner, the nun's priest, the nun. The pilgrims were complex, creative, and often, corrupt. I was unsure what the reaction would be in a Catholic school. The Director of Studies, a Christian Brother, stopped by with the Religion Department chair. They discussed the work with the students. Conversations buzzed—punctuated with passionate defenses of one or another point followed by laughter and listening—on both sides.

The administrators moved toward the door as the long block period ended. The students fell silent. Uneasy.

"Good work," said the chair. "Provocative. Defensible. Courageous." The students began high-fiving and whistling. All this energy around a 700-year-old text.

Paulo Freire. The golden key.

Part Four

CULTIVATE AND COACH

WHAT IS BEST DESIGN STRATEGY?

Few truths have been as well established by research as the fact that most of what we learn during our lives is learned by imitation. We see things done and we try to do likewise.
—Robert F. Mager

CHAPTER EIGHT

THE QUEEN'S CROQUET GROUND

None of us got where we are solely by pulling ourselves up by our bootstraps. We got here because somebody—a parent, a teacher, an Ivy League crony, or a few nuns—bent down and helped us pick up our boots.
—Thurgood Marshall

"That's right, Five! Always lay the blame on others!"
"You'd better not talk!" said Five. "I heard the Queen say only yesterday you deserved to be beheaded."
"What for?" said the one who had spoken first.
"That's none of your business, Two!" said Seven.
"Yes, it is his business!" said Five. "And I'll tell him—it was for bringing the cook tulip-roots instead of onions."
—Chapter Eight,
Alice's Adventures in Wonderland

PRECISION TOOLS

Multiple meanings. Sometimes they're intentional. Intriguing. Inspiring. Other times they're careless. Confusing. Even catastrophic. Words slip and slide. Scoot out of reach. Leave chaos behind. The Wonderland cook wanted onions. Tulip roots were close. Not close enough. Likewise with words. Subtle differences matter.

How to teach writing? Wrong question. "Why" is first. Like the distinction in skating between compulsory figures and free skate, writing changes form depending on purpose and audience. The school offered many upper-division electives. I developed more to broaden the landscape. Among them—Professional and Scholarly Writing and Technical Writing. In both the goal was a technical manual—either analytical or informational.

The classes focused on creating documents that reflected compulsive care and competence. "I want you to look at these projects 30 years from now and say, 'WOW! Look what I did!'" I said as I passed out the detailed specs.

The manuals ranged to a hundred pages or more. Students indexed them to a technical-writing textbook so every writing strategy and technique could be found in their project. There were proposals and rationales, timelines, data-based conclusions, abstracts, summaries, graphics, implementation plans or areas for further study. They bound their work at the local copy shop. With vinyl covers and coil spines the projects looked as professional as they were. In formal presentations at the end of the term one copy went to the library. One to the person or business most helpful in their research. One they kept for themselves.

The first requirement: a topic important to them. It became a clue to many futures. Scooter Barry, son of basketball great Rick Barry, wrote a detailed, diagrammed manual on the fundamentals of basketball. He attached a note. "Mrs. Koch—People can use this to understand my sport better. Look for me at Kansas." I used it several years later as he led the Jayhawks to the NCAA Championship. He was right. The manual helped me understand the weaving patterns and rapid ball handling with new appreciation.

Another student wrote about "The Impact of the Breakup of AT&T on the Telecommunication Industry." An unusual topic, I thought then. Maybe not. Today he is a CEO.

There were employee manuals for small businesses, dental practices, real estate offices. Analyses of job prospects in law, the future of blacksmithing (by a student who became one despite all odds), promotional strategies for non-profit childcare centers, inventory protocols for local theater companies, templates to classify graffiti patterns around their city. I learned about topics I never would have assigned on my own.

Classwork targeted specific skills. Clear thinking. Logic. Readability. We made paper airplanes. Flew them. Wrote the steps so someone else could construct the same plane. The room transformed from calm to chaotic at every launch. Crashes were routine. Designers were critical. Builders were defensive.

"How could you do that?" one would say.

"I just did what you wrote down," another would retort.

"You're supposed to use common sense."

"Yeah, well how much common sense do you see anywhere?"

I would intervene. "Start again. You're not finished until it flies. Then switch roles."

We repeated the exercise with peanut-butter sandwiches. More than a few students stood helplessly in front of the jars when directions failed to tell them to "twist the lid to open."

We drew maps to campus destinations and tried to follow them. Students wandered everywhere. I trusted them to come back. They did. Today students are monitored and micro-managed. I suspect no one is wandering around any campus unsupervised with a hand-drawn map to a light pole. Or to anything else. Probably no peanut-butter sandwiches either. Food allergies. Schools are terrified of lawsuits. It may be tidier. It's definitely more tedious.

I brought baskets of apples, or lemons, or potatoes. Students described them, put them back, then tried to find their own. We spent hours on ambiguous word meanings—"good," "soap," "run," "long"—countless others. Most words are ambiguous. We read George Orwell. Studied advertisements for faulty reasoning and propaganda techniques. Wrote a thousand words on the relationship of thought and language.

Sean Anderson is a biology professor at Cal State Channel Islands. In 1986 he was a writer for the school paper, *Les Hommes de Foi*. Sean wrote an article with the grim title "Does Koch Equal Death?" After several paragraphs detailing a "depressing list of features: no breaks, constant work, big projects"—he ends:

"Perhaps the only redeeming quality of her class (aside from finishing it) is what you learn. For example, Gerry Armentrout took her Professional and Scholarly Writing Class. He saved his binder and took it with him to MIT. For his first-year English class he used it for a study guide. While others were getting C's and D's, he got an A–. She might be hard, but she cares. She's with you the whole term. Maybe it's not death. It might be life. Decide for yourself."

Amanda Ripley is an investigative journalist for *Time* magazine and *The Atlantic*. She writes about human behavior and public policy. In 2013 she released her newest book, *The Smartest Kids in the World*, about her global quest to discover how other countries build smarter kids.

Ripley reports our schools aren't doing well against other nations. Controlling for income among the richest quartile we rank 21st in math, 23rd in science. After a year of research and travel she concluded, "Many of our students can't solve problems they've never seen before. Their critical thinking skills are weak. The focus is on test-taking."

Yet the top three performing countries in the world today (South

Korea, Finland, and Poland) didn't always have good schools. What happened? She says excellent schools don't depend on technology, though it helps. "America has been seduced by a massive marketing machine. It's a frenzy disconnected from reality. Actually, it is an attempt to create a parallel reality." Three things characterized successful schools in her study:

(1). School is hard. Much harder than here.

(2). Sports are a hobby.

(3). Students know there is something in it for them.

While the gardeners in Wonderland are arguing and blaming one another, they hear the sound of many footsteps approaching. They throw themselves flat on their faces. The Queen is coming.

Schools are the same. While politicians, pundits, and parents argue and blame one another for schools that don't work, there are footsteps here as well. It is the sound of students leaving places that let them down. Walking away from their futures.

Amanda Ripley may be right about what makes good schools. But great schools have two other elements—care and compassion.

I didn't wait for the Queen to tell us what to do. I knew. It always came back to the same lessons. Love them. Listen to them. Lead them. Then walk beside them. Then let them walk ahead. Expect their best. Give yours.

Sean wasn't quite right when he wrote, "She's with you the whole way."

I wasn't with them. We were with each other. Considering. Collecting. Choosing exact words to convey meaning.

Precision tools.

"How are you getting on?" said the Cat, as soon as there was mouth enough for it to speak with.

Alice waited till the eyes appeared, and then nodded. "It's no use speaking to it," she thought, "till its ears have come, or at least one of them." In another minute the whole head appeared, and then Alice put down her flamingo, and began an account of the game... "You've no idea how confusing it all is the things being alive: for instance, there's the arch I've got to go through next walking about at the other end of the ground—and I should have croqueted the Queen's hedgehog just now, only it ran away when it saw mine coming!"

—Chapter Eight,
Alice's Adventures in Wonderland

THROUGH DIFFERENT EYES

Writer Ann Patchett says her idea of a productive day is "reading for hours and staring out the window." She is not alone. There are many explanations for this behavior. Some are lofty. Alice McDermott, in *Confessions of a Reluctant Catholic*, says about her love of reading, "Fiction makes chaos bearable. It transforms the fleeting stuff of daily life." I had another reason. More mundane. Reading is fun. Most days I wore a large black lapel button to school. It proclaimed "READING IS FUN— DAMENTAL!" I was a walking bumper sticker. Bumper stickers don't convert automobile drivers. They annoy them. My lapel button had the same effect on my students. I wondered. Why weren't they having fun?

Like most teachers, I assigned reading. Often by chapters. There were study questions. For a time I required journals. What were they thinking? What didn't they understand? It was clear the work was still a chore.

After yet another round of "Let's look at the study questions and journal entries" a sullen boy in back of the class raised his hand.

"I'm sick of journals. Come on, Mrs. Koch. We need a break. I have one in every class. We're even doing them in PE. I can't keep up."

That's another problem schools have. Every teacher forgets they're not the only actor in the play.

"Yeah, he's right" echoed others. "I don't get this 'levels of meaning' crap," said someone else. "Most of us have a huge biology project due Monday. I don't care about these fake stories."

A little mutiny on my hands.

"Okay. Let me think about this. No reading at home the rest of the week. Do your biology projects."

Teenagers aren't alone in discounting literature. I took a a 10-week undergraduate course at UCLA—"The Sentence." When my future husband looked at my class schedule his eyes narrowed.

"'The Sentence'? You're spending a whole quarter on THE SEN-TENCE?" He shook his head in disbelief.

"Subject. Verb. Complete thought. That's it. What else is there to say?" he said smugly.

There's a lot more to say. I spent the term interrupting his factor-analysis study by dropping tidbits about the sentence. He wasn't happy. In self defense he said, "You win. How do people develop the skills to read more than the obvious?" Good question.

Decoding print used to be the job of K-3 teachers in California. Then somehow students were expected to leap to deeper comprehension by osmosis. Decoding is part of reading—the first part. Not the only part. By the time students get to high school every one assumes they can read. They can decode. It's not the same thing.

The rest of the week the students were delighted. No study questions. No journals. Not even a quiz. We concentrated on vocabulary words they didn't know. They made their own lists from the book we were reading. The technique was to use the context the word appeared in to help them figure out the meaning without looking it up. It was small-scale detective work. They were reading, just not pages and pages. Single paragraphs.

I love graphic art. Comic books. Comic strips. Editorial-page satirical drawings. *New Yorker* cartoons. Propping the newspaper comics against the milk carton the next weekend, I thought, "That's it! I need something shorter for us to practice on. Comic strips are perfect."

Bill Watterson had just begun drawing "Calvin and Hobbes"—his imaginary world where a six-year-old boy and a stuffed tiger lived. A tiger who is alive in Calvin's mind, even if nowhere else. Calvin asked questions about big issues—Hobbes had answers. He helped Calvin find others on his own. Hobbes was much smarter than Calvin's teacher, Miss Wormwood, who never had answers. Who was annoyed by questions. She was counting the days until retirement—five years to go. She taught in every school I worked in. Every school I attended. We all know her.

I began bringing two or three Watterson strips to class every week. They became a Monday staple. I Xeroxed them. Under each strip I spaced three words: literal, inferential, applied. We worked through frames together. We recorded the literal. What do you see? They didn't see the same things. The differences surprised them. Once we mastered description we turned to inferences. The strips were a perfect vehicle for helping people move from one level to another in the reading process.

Students defended their ideas. "Are you crazy?" they would say to classmates with different points of view, launching into detailed connections between what the characters were doing and how they drew their conclusions. The third level—"how does it connect to you?"—was easier. The graphic form gave them confidence.

Students got better. Their answers became more detailed, more grounded, more astute. They were doing more than decoding. I abandoned journals and lengthy study questions. I returned to assigned reading with simpler requests: "Be ready to share two or three inferences from tonight's assignment." Or "What happened? How do you feel about that?"

On New Year's Eve, 1995, Watterson published his last "Calvin and Hobbes." He had drawn 3160 strips. They appeared in 2300 publications worldwide. On the final day the little boy and his beloved tiger are sledding down a long hill. The last frame is empty. They have gone on to new adventures. That year my students wrote moving, thoughtful essays about where those adventures might be. The characters were no longer in "fake stories." They were real.

A dozen years later I opened a letter from a former student. Matt had become a high school history teacher. He sent his course outline. At the bottom was a cartoon. "Look, Mrs. Koch," his note said. "Recognize anything?"

Calvin and Hobbes are gone. They're not forgotten. Someone else is sledding now. Asking questions. Looking beyond the obvious. Learning to read.

Having fun.

"Who are you talking to?" said the King, coming up to Alice, and looking at the Cat's head with great curiosity.

"It's a friend of mine—a Cheshire-Cat," said Alice: "allow me to introduce it."

"I don't like the look of it at all," said the King. "It must be removed."

He called to the Queen, who was passing at the moment. "My dear! I wish you would have this cat removed!"

The Queen had only one way of settling all difficulties, great or small. "Off with his head!" she said without even looking around.

—Chapter Eight,
Alice's Adventures in Wonderland

INDEPENDENT MINDS

The memo in the faculty mailbox was marked URGENT. CALL PARENT IMMEDIATELY. VERY ANGRY. "Very" was underlined multiple times.

I sighed. Teachers can't respond immediately. They don't work alone. They are lucky to have five minutes to themselves between the start of school and the last bell. Parents have to wait. Most of us tried to respond the same day. In the time before technology hijacked communication and called it convenience, I jammed the green paper notice in my pocket. After school was the best I could do.

The student whose parent called was in my sixth-period class. He strolled in, dropped his book bag, and took off his letterman's jacket.

"Hi Paul. Is everything okay?"

"Sure, Mrs. K. Why?"

"Your mom called. Any ideas?"

"Yeah," he shrugged. "I'm not going to read the next book. My parents don't approve. She'll explain."

Last period ended at 2:55. I called at three o'clock. I barely identified myself before a shrill voice interrupted. "What took you

136

so long?" Not waiting for an answer, she launched into a series of rapid-fire questions. I realized no answers were expected. It was like dodging bullets.

"Do you realize this IS a CATHOLIC school?"

"Do you understand your job is to PROTECT children from evil?"

"Don't you have better things to do than teach trash?"

"Don't you know *The Chocolate War* is a banned book?"

So that was it. The American Library Association promotes Banned Book Week every year to draw attention to the freedom to read. The list reports where and what is being banned by citizen committees, school boards, church groups. Over time the list has included everyone from Kingsley Amis to Walt Whitman. Steinbeck, Hemmingway, Orwell, Tolkien are all there. Over the last 30 years 11,000 books have appeared. In 2009 *Harry Potter* was number one. Most of the books I taught were on the list: *To Kill a Mockingbird*, *Lord of the Flies*, and the one that triggered the phone call: Robert Cormier's *The Chocolate War*.

"Let's meet face to face," I said when she wound down.

"I can't come to school. I have a young child."

"No problem. I will come to your house. Is today convenient? The unit starts tomorrow."

I arrived at 4:30. What followed wasn't a discussion. It was a lecture.

"This book doesn't end happily," she said, waving it under my nose. "Children need happy endings. AND, it shows religious figures in a bad light." She glared as if I had written the book myself to corrupt her son.

I took out the project I intended to assign. As all my projects did, it had the reasons why we were doing the work at the top. I handed it to her.

She read it. "Absolutely not. If you can't come up with another project I'm calling the principal. In fact, I'm going to call him anyway."

I was tired. I had my own children waiting at home. I made a last stab at placating her.

"What passages do you object to?"

She sniffed. "I haven't read the book. I've heard about it."

There was no way to respond. I said, "I'm disappointed. I would never teach something destructive. Your son is 15. Do you have any idea the world he lives in every day? I'm not going to make a special assignment for him. Since you are calling the school anyway, ask if he can spend a couple of weeks in the library."

As I rose to leave, she called after me, "Be sure you shut the door so the baby doesn't get out." Slamming it harder than I needed to I muttered, "And no ideas can get in either."

The boy missed the unit. For families like his the point of the Bible is to provide divine knowledge for guiding our lives. We don't need questioning or critical thinking. Yet anyone who reads the Old Testament, even a little, sees people who maintain their capacity for independent thought. Some are disobedient. Even contentious. Abraham, Isaac, Jacob all confront authority and break laws. And they're praised. It didn't seem worth mentioning.

He returned after the exam. His classmates' work hung everywhere. Collages capturing complex personalities. Plot outlines. Charts detailing the influence of advertising on sales. Large posters generalizing the book events to real life.

We never spoke about his absence. I adjusted the grade total score so he wasn't penalized for the missing assignments. I left the work up longer than usual. Many times that spring I saw him "reading" the walls.

As Alice travels through Wonderland she learns that learning to play its games is more than learning the rules. I was learning too. My student may have missed the classwork.

He didn't miss the point.

At least I hope not.

CHAPTER NINE

THE MOCK TURTLE'S STORY

Any place that anyone young can learn something useful from
someone with experience is an educational institution.
—Al Capp

"You can't think how glad I am to see you again, you dear old
thing!" said the Duchess, as she tucked her arm affectionately into
Alice's, and they walked off together.
Alice was glad to find her in such a pleasant temper, and thought
to herself that perhaps it was only the pepper that had made her so
savage when they met in the kitchen.
"When I'm a Duchess," she said to herself, "I won't have any pepper
in my kitchen at all. Maybe it's always pepper that makes people
hot-tempered," she went on, very much pleased at having found out
a new kind of rule, "and vinegar makes them sour—and chamo-
mile makes them bitter—and—and barley sugar and such things
that make children sweet-tempered. I only wish people knew that:
then they wouldn't be so stingy about it, you know—"
—Chapter Nine,
Alice's Adventures in Wonderland

COOKING SECRETS

School days fly by like calendar pages that disappear one by
one in old-fashioned movies. The bonds forged through hours

together—hours of conversation, challenge, collapse, conquest—
come to an end. Fall classes have spring replacements. Year-long
subjects wind up in June. Students often left farewell notes—on
my desk, in my faculty mailbox, beneath the car windshield wiper,
under the classroom door. I taught many of them in more than one
course. For some we had spent a thousand hours together—in class,
after school, working on projects at their homes, in the library, at
my own kitchen table.

> *Thanks for being a teacher, mother, and friend. And 'she worked
> so well with her hands'...See, my variation on Willy Loman.
> Seriously, over the last three years Daryle and I have griped at
> you, begged you, bugged you, pestered you, kept you awake at
> all hours, bored you, and surprised you (not necessarily in that
> order). We can't do anything tangible for you but keep on learn-
> ing. I think that's what you wanted all along. Thanks for caring
> about us. – Paulette*

> *It's been three years of papers, projects, poems, 'You don't have to
> write this down,' hugs, and generally challenging, thought inspir-
> ing work. Never a dull moment, but an occasional crummy paper.
> I've done work I am truly proud of, and I can now more than
> ever understand the meaning of what I've learned. Forgive me
> if I don't come back to visit. I hate sentimental remembrances
> and long good-byes. – Geoff*

> *Can you believe we made it through alive? After three years I can
> truthfully say I'm going to miss biting my nails to the quick at
> four in the morning. I'll carry what I've learned forever. Thank
> you. Love, Sean*

> *It's all over. In a weird way I enjoyed this stress. I couldn't have
> made it without the hugs. I never can write as much as I want
> to—you know that—you read my work. Thanks a lot. I will
> bring you a Santa Cruz shirt. Love, Andy*

I am glad this class is over. It's the hardest class I've ever been through—but I learned a lot—surprise. I can't say that about most high school classes. And hey—it provided time for Ann, Madeleine, and me to spend most of our time for weeks together and say, 'Okay, now we need to stop talking and finish this part tonight..' Your kindness made it worth it. Love, Justine

You made me depressed, you made me stressed, and you made me cry. But there is one thing no one else ever did that you pushed me to do. You made me work. I thank you for this. Love, Ann

To the woman who took me to Hell (and made me pay her a dime every time I swore in class...now I owe you again). Thanks for the memories. Look up in the sky. One day a jet could be sky writing my thanks. Sincerely and always your student, Ruben (USNR)

The Duchess is one of the most unpleasant characters in Wonderland. She is volatile, dangerous, opinionated. Worst, she is given to moralizing.

> *"You're thinking about something, my dear, and that makes you forget to talk. I can't tell you just now what the moral of that is, but I shall remember it in a bit."*
> *"Perhaps it hasn't one," Alice ventured to remark.*
> *"Tut, tut, child!" said the Duchess. "Everything's got a moral, if only you can find it."*

When Alice remains quiet the Duchess asks, "Thinking again?" with a dig of her sharp chin into Alice's shoulder.

> *"I've a right to think," said Alice sharply, for she was beginning to feel a little worried.*
> *"Just about as much right," said the Duchess, "as pigs have to fly; and the m—"*

Sometimes schools are the Duchess's kitchen—places full of mental fog like the smoke that hovered end-to-end in the large room. Where assignments underestimate student potential. "You don't know much," said the Duchess, "and that's a fact." Where classes are "filled with extraordinary noise—a constant howling and sneezing and every now and then a great crash." Where students feel confused.

Years of experimentation together with some extraordinary master chefs who mentored me resulted in a simple recipe:

Before you begin:
Make sure everyone has the tools they need.
Plan for different appetites.
Mix well:
Less pepper.
More sugar.
Less talk.
More kindness.
Add:
Less unsupported opinion.
More careful exposition.
Less competition.
More cooperation.
Fold in:
Experiments.
Unexpected opportunities.
Student opinions.
Tips:
Avoid sharp chins.
Adjust oven temperature as needed.
Take time.
Sprinkle liberally with hugs.
Serves any size group.

Time and hugs. Both are in short supply in schools today. Modern recipes are different. Faster. Designed by others. Easy to download. Nutritious—probably. Nurturing—less so.

There's never a substitute for love.

Alice turned to the Mock Turtle and said, "What else had you to learn?"
"Well, there was Mystery," the Mock Turtle replied…
"and Laughing and Grief."
—Chapter Nine
Alice's Adventures in Wonderland

What Else Had You to Learn?

Teenagers know a lot. We forget. Literature books are filled with complicated characters and big ideas—heroes and villains, wise men and fools. Success. Failure. Hypocrisy. Integrity. What if students could pick their own book to share? A book that mattered to them. A book not prescribed by someone else? I began a program called Senior Orals.

The directions: If you could share one book with a friend who needed a boost, what would it be? One page. Due any time this year. Bring the book. Read a passage to us before you read the recommendation.

The months passed. Students would pop up. "I've got my Senior Oral ready!" We would stop. Listen. Applaud. Like the mysterious way potluck dinners work even without assigned food categories, their choices added texture and variety to the traditional canon we were absorbed in. They became another thread weaving us together—a community of learners.

I assembled their work in a pamphlet I gave each person at the end of every year. We called it "A Reader's Delight." Because it was. Some ended like this:

If I had a friend who needed to remember heroes do more than what is asked of them, and there are lots of ways to make society better, I would tell him to read Star Wars—The Last Command. *No barrier is unbreakable if you set your mind to it. – Brian*

If I had a friend who gave of himself for those he loved, I would give him this wonderful book—Shel Silverstein's The Giving Tree. *From it I learned the lesson of giving more than taking. It reminds me of my parents. I am giving them the story this Christmas. – Diana*

I'd love to make everyone read this book. Read it when your parents disturb you and then quote from it at the dinner table. Read it when your goldfish dies. Read it so you can say you've heard of Ring Lardner. It's not a book. It's a state of mind. It's Franny and Zooey *by J.D. Salinger. – Bekki*

If I had a friend who needed to remember not to take life for granted, to take time to smell the flowers, to remember what is important—sunsets, seasons, families, time itself—I would recommend Thornton Wilder's Our Town. *– Kathleen*

It was the kind of thing when I finished reading that I just thought to myself…cool. The way we judge people is kind of funny. A lot of people would see these guys as losers or bums, but I saw them as people who knew what they wanted in life— nothing—and they excelled at it. Maybe being the bottom of the barrel isn't so bad. There it is easy to relate and be nice to each other. I think if we created a common ground for people to roam, it would make life more pleasant for everyone. If I had a friend who was sort of down and needed to feel more hopeful, I'd recommend John Steinbeck's Cannery Row. *I did have that friend. He was me. – Josh*

Hundreds of students completed Senior Orals. I sat in back. They stood in front. They taught one another. They taught me.

Big ideas aren't big because the writers are famous. They are big because they tell the human story. Students know that.

It's their story too.

*"And how many hours a day did you do lessons?" said Alice.
"Ten hours the first day," said the Mock Turtle: "nine the next, and
so on."
"What a curious plan!" exclaimed Alice.
"That's the reason they're called lesson," the Gryphon remarked:
"because they lessen from day to day."
This was quite a new idea to Alice, and she thought it over before
she made her next remark. "Then the eleventh day must have been
a holiday?"
"Of course it was," said the Mock Turtle.
"And how did you manage on the twelfth?" Alice went on eagerly.
"That's enough about lessons," the Gryphon interrupted.*
—Chapter Nine
Alice's Adventures in Wonderland

THE TWELFTH DAY

*T*eachers run out of time before they run out of things they
hoped to do and now never will—at least with the class
they're looking at in June. It is like growing old, but for teachers
old age arrives every year. As students crossed the stage in their
caps and gowns I struggled with hope and despair. I wondered,
What else could I have done? Are they ready?

Endings. Sometimes we know we're facing one. Sometimes we
don't. Graduations were in my "we know it's over" column. Students
move on. They disappear like Harry Potter leaving Station 9 ¾ for
the last time.

We heard about former students through the grapevine that ties
school communities together—younger siblings, alumni newsletters,
the graduates themselves. Sometimes someone would appear at my
classroom door unexpectedly. Adjusting my eyesight the years slipped
away, and I could see the teenager I taught in the adult standing

before me.

Scott was one. A tall, shy boy, he wanted to be an engineer. We spent months talking about pros and cons. He sailed through Technical Writing. In his senior year he signed up for Advanced Placement English. The writing was different. The curriculum broader. The books raised more questions than they answered. He was intrigued. We spent hours talking about ideas. Hours revising his work. His family encouraged him. So did I. "But I'm a math guy," he would say.

"You never know. Engineers write too. They manage other engineers. After all this you'll know what to do when you're dealing with strange personality types, right? Besides, you might not always be an engineer. You're taking this class, aren't you?"

His crooked smile would light up his face. Scott went to Cal Poly, graduated, and landed a job with a good engineering firm. Several years later he came to see me. "Engineering is okay," he said, "but I don't want to do it forever. I'm going to law school."

"Great. Now you'll have a chance to see King Lear in action. You'll know what to do. Elder abuse. Harassment. Property rights. Trespassing. Perjury. Assault. Murder. It's all there."

He laughed. "I doubt I'll meet anyone so colorful."

The talented boy I knew had become a young man with another dream—a twelfth-day dream.

Twenty years passed. A letter arrived.

Poling and Poling
Attorneys at Law
Martinez, California
February 3, 2006
Dear Anne:
I hope this letter finds you well.
It has been so long since we last talked. I am not sure you remember the tall lanky kid from your AP English class (1986).

Something reminded me today of the many different people who had an impact on my life, and I was moved to jot you this note. My son Luke is now in the sixth grade. As he approaches high school, I hope he will be fortunate enough to encounter someone similar.

Please give my best to your family. From the letterhead you have probably gathered that my mother and law partner is still going strong. I am working on Probate, Conservatorship, and Elder Law issues.

If you have a chance, please drop me a note and let me know how you are doing.

Sincerely,

Scott

We met for lunch. I didn't recognize the tall distinguished man in the sport coat and tie. I did recognize the boyish smile. We laughed, talked, reminisced. As we walked out he turned, "You know, I have met Lear's daughters. I've met Lear too. More than once. Pretty scary."

"But you recognized them, right?"

"Every time."

We've always had great hopes for our schools. Thomas Jefferson imagined an aristocracy of intellect. Horace Mann imagined universal education to roll the wheel of progress. James Bryant Conant, President of Harvard from the end of World War II to the mid 1960s, imagined schools would answer the threat of Soviet Russia. Catholic bishops imagined a place where students would be protected from religious discrimination and trained to remain loyal to the Church.

It never quite works out like we imagine. But we still hope. Theologian Gabriel Marcel says, "Hope is not a denial of the facts of life but an expression of them."

The Wonderland creatures went to school under the sea. Alice wonders how they managed on twelfth day. The answer…very well. When lessons were over they kept learning—in new places, from new people, for different reasons. So do students.

School ends whether we achieve what we hoped for or not. But I was wrong about graduation. It isn't THE end. It's the eleventh day. My colleagues and I taught students who became teachers, coaches, dentists, doctors, priests, lawyers, policemen, sheriffs, firemen, military men, CEO's, middle managers, scientists, small business owners, insurance salesmen, real estate brokers, pilots.

Tom and Derek became geologists. Joe drove a garbage truck. Clayton opened an architecture practice. Kent led a software start-up. Matt signed on to crew with America's Cup. Richard an accountant. Kyle became an Oregon newscaster. Sean a college basketball announcer. Kevin an investment banker. Toby a foreign service officer. Damian and Sean college professors.

One became a paramedic. Some took over family businesses—car dealerships, restaurants, landscape services. Several became journalists. One a botanist. One a blacksmith. At least two psychologists. Some became engineers. Freelance writers. Counselors. Software developers. A few became professional athletes. The list was as varied as they were.

Their journeys simply began in school. Over time I despaired less over what I hadn't done. We did a great deal. A great deal remained undone. That's what living is.

A single teacher plays only a small part of any student's life. On the other hand, students are a huge part of a teacher's world.

On the first eleven days, and on the twelfth, Scott was one part of mine.

Part Five

CALIBRATE

DID IT WORK?

A powerful way to organize is to build around a meaningful out-come. When students can understand and experience the need for the instruction, they are likely to be more highly motivated, learn better, and retain longer.
—Robert F. Mager

CHAPTER TEN

THE LOBSTER QUADRILLE

"To think is to differ."
—Clarence Darrow

So they began solemnly dancing round and round Alice, every now and then treading on her toes when they passed too close...while the Mock Turtle sang this, very slowly and sadly:—
"Will you walk a little faster?" said a whiting to a snail,
"There's a porpoise close behind us, and he's treading on my tail.
See how eagerly the lobsters and turtles all advance!
They are waiting on the shingle—will you come and join the dance?"
—Chapter Ten
Alice's Adventures in Wonderland

JOIN THE DANCE?

The course had an awkward title—"Writing: Process and Product." It targeted students who either struggled with writing or weren't interested in writing. Some weren't interested in school...period.

The course description said students would cover various writing forms: description, narration, research, and personal essay. It sounded like a tedious march through a stylized word wasteland. For them.

For me.

For several years I doggedly followed the curriculum directions. Used the trendy mantra that echoes in writing instruction: "show, don't tell." The results were disappointing. Putting the reader in a scene rather than telling them about it is useful. But in the end it can be just as enervating as dry narration. How much detail is enough? How much distracts readers from authentic emotional exploration or careful exposition?

Jerry sat near the door. Every time it opened he stared wistfully out. Nick cowered in the back corner. The first week neither boy took off his coat, as though they weren't planning to stay. On opening day I assigned a "free write" in class. "Write anything," I said. "Keep the pen moving on the paper for ten minutes."

After school I looked over the responses. Jerry's paper was blank. His name hovered in tiny print at the top. Nick's work was barely readable. A childish printing with almost every word misspelled staggered down the page.

I went to the office. The Director of Studies looked up.

"Look at this," I ranted. "These boys are 17 years old. How have they gotten this far?"

The tired administrator studied the papers. "The reason is obvious," he said. "They can't read. And one of them can barely write."

"How can we let them graduate next year?"

"One has parents who have assured us they want him to experience as much as he can. They know his limitations. He'll work in their family business. As for the other one, do what you can. Any more questions?"

I felt frustrated. Like a fraud. What were we doing? How does someone stay in school and never learn to read or write? I went home and tore up the course outline. I needed a new approach. My usual routine, a series of assignments beginning with a personal essay and ending with a research paper, had seemed a logical idea. It hadn't worked for three years. Why did it take me so long to get the message? The answer—denial. It's not uncommon. Teachers are too busy, too tired, too stressed to redo every thing that doesn't work.

Jerry and Nick weren't the only students with problems. Theirs were just more severe than most. I didn't know these students or their classmates. I needed to. Students don't come in standard sizes like shoes. "Bad" students are bad in different ways just as good students are. Students are individuals. Individual implies unique. In the classroom that implication is born out as fact.

In my commuter high school students came from different cities, different socio-economic backgrounds, and despite being a Catholic institution, different religions.

I wondered. How could I make their differences an asset?

A researcher at the University of Western Ontario, Allan Paivio, developed a concept he called "dual coding theory" in the early 1970s. His idea: if instruction gives equal weight to verbal and non-verbal cues, students are more likely to remember and understand material. I used it often in literature classes. It works. Would it work in a writing class?

I rewrote the course around what I called "The Place Project." Students focused on where they lived. What did it look like? What made it home? When they shut their eyes what did they see? Where were their favorite places? I asked them to bring snapshots. Hunt for magazines pictures that reminded them of their towns. Soon the walls were covered with images, drawings, maps, even a birdhouse one student retrieved from his garage. In four parts the writing components focused on the history of their place, a description of their favorite spot, an interview with a longtime resident, and finally, a personal essay that included how they were influenced by where they lived.

I stuck to the primary characteristics of each form. I invited people for them to practice interviewing—a baker, a volunteer at a wildlife museum, a veterinarian, an attorney, a park ranger. Students read their work to each other. There were two rules. No badgering. No blowing off the classwork. My promise—if the classwork went well no other homework. They were hooked. Good students often work on longer assignments. Average students are tormented with daily demands. It's a subtle message but a destructive one. You're not smart enough to handle more. Daily practice doesn't have to be at home. Actually, home is the worst place.

During final exam week, every student spoke about how "place" had influenced them. The room was still. The students connected. Their different worlds turned out not to be so different after all.

Jerry and Nick both passed. They recorded their interviews. Wrote short captions under their favorite place pictures. Drew timelines of their city histories. I met with Jerry to discuss how his city influenced him. Nick wrote a personal essay. We revised it together a dozen times.

He commuted from Livermore, a city home to a famous national science lab. In his essay he wrote, "A physicist at the lab told me the value of a scientist lies not in the answers he finds, but questions he asks. I know I'm not a good writer, but I'm better than I thought. Thanks for making it okay to ask questions…and for giving me some choices."

When the Mock Turtle sings to Alice about joining the dance, she is not the only one who hesitates.

…the snail replied "Too far, too far!" And gave a look askance—
Said he thanked the whiting kindly, but he would not join the
dance.

The "dance" called college preparatory education is not for everyone. It is odd that we think it is. In 1870 only two percent of 17-year-olds graduated from high school. There were many ways to learn outside the narrow confines of a classical education. Both Jerry and Nick would have benefitted from something else.

I used "The Place Project" as long as I taught the course. Most students joined the dance…one way or another.

For some the "admission ticket" was the text-based project. For others it was a collection like Nick's. For a few it was images and conversation like Jerry's. I couldn't change the system. I could make sure everyone had a chance.

The course title turned out to be better than I thought. Writing is a process. The product—usually words, but not exclusively. It's also discovery and understanding.

Two boys who hated writing reminded me.

"I could tell you my adventures—beginning from this morning,"
said Alice a little timidly; "but it's no use going back to yesterday,
because I was a different person then."
"Explain all that," said the Mock Turtle.
"No, no! The adventures first," said the Gryphon in an impatient
tone: "explanations take such a dreadful time."
—Chapter Ten
Alice's Adventures in Wonderland

ADVENTURES FIRST

W riter Joan Didion observed, "We are well advised to keep on nodding terms with the people we used to be, whether we find them attractive company or not." The same is true for education policy makers.

At the beginning of 2013 California Superintendent of Public Instruction Tom Torlakson made an announcement. "We are proposing revising our state STAR testing required of all students. Multiple choice tests cannot do the job anymore. We are going to include in-depth essays that test critical thinking beginning in 2015. Schools need to teach more than facts testing recall." The news was heralded as a "breakthrough" in education practice. The problem? It's not a breakthrough.

Teaching critical thinking is a voguish concept. It stands with "multiple intelligences" and "learning styles" at the forefront of educational practice. Politicians and professionals alike talk about the need for critical thinking in a globalized world as though it is a revolutionary idea.

When an elderly aunt who taught school for 39 years died three decades ago, I inherited her books. One was a heavy leather volume—*The Classroom Teacher*, edited by Lewis Terman. Terman developed the Stanford-Binet IQ tests, chaired the Stanford psychology department for 23 years, and devoted his career to measuring achievement.

The book begins, "The aims of teaching reading have changed radically since 1910. Today thoughtful teachers now consider reading as a means of extending the experiences of boys and girls, of stimulating good thinking, and of arousing interest in a wide variety of reading activities. Teachers teach to find the author's aim, identify important ideas, draw valid conclusions, judge the validity of statements, discover problems for additional study." The list is critical thinking skills minus the label. The copyright date—1927.

Students can't apply critical thinking skills by any name unless they understand the material. Time-consuming, tedious work. Experience taught me clever students can talk about anything and make it look like thinking. But if they don't understand the content the analysis doesn't hold up.

William Shakespeare. The name conjures two responses from adults—horror first followed by some variation on "Yes, he certainly IS a genius." From students the reaction is reluctance morphing to revolt. All the big ideas are there—love, revenge, war. Sex. Students didn't care. They couldn't decipher it. Reading strategies, i.e., identify main ideas and write critical responses—are futile if you don't know enough facts to fill in what is left unsaid.

Winter term meant "King Lear." It was a slog. After half a dozen years of parsing, pleading, pushing, I thought, What am I doing? The answer—ruining a great play. It was a frequent Advanced Placement exam topic. I decided no more botched reading aloud. No more opening lectures on the nature of tragedy. No more personal essays on family obligations. So now what?

Sir Laurence Olivier's performance of "King Lear" had become available on VHS. I bought it. Teachers know popping in videos and expecting anything good to happen is a fantasy. Nevertheless, I taught with a few people who did that, whether it fit the curriculum or not.

But I wanted the students to see "Lear" all in one sitting in a place I could pause it whenever they were confused---which is to say every few minutes. Even in a 90-minute block schedule I didn't have time for the three-hour production at school.

"'Lear' begins in two weeks," I said. "I've got the movie. Let's watch it together before we get started. You're invited to my house next Sunday. 5 o'clock."

Voices rang out.

"Your house?"

"On a weekend?"

"That's dinner time."

"No problem," I said. "I'll fix lasagna. Plan on it."

They were aggravated. Apprehensive. In the end it was an adventure they couldn't resist. I spent hours cooking. At the appointed time they descended—30 self-conscious curious teenagers. Soon sprawled everywhere. The family room looked like old VW Beetle stunts for how many people can you cram in a small space.

"I'm beat," some said.

"Take a nap. I'll wake you for the good parts."

"OK, here we go. We'll stop every few minutes and debrief." I wondered if this was like coaches breaking down film after football games. Or scouting next week's opponent. Maybe.

It worked. Between the Italian food and the comfort of a home, we managed to sort out things they would never have asked in class.

The basic questions—"Who IS that?" "What did he just say?" "What's going on now?"

The honest reactions—"That dude just had his eyes pulled out—gross." "The guy is nuts." "This reminds me of my sisters."

My favorite—"Where is Mrs. Lear? Her husband is clueless."

The "Lasagna with Lear" dinner became a yearly staple. Afterwards I took the tape to school. We'd watch key scenes over and over—sometimes half a dozen times. Students acted out the "pity and terror" they understood better because they understood the language, the plot, the context. They made videos. One memorable year, the characters were Legos moved by an unseen hand and attacked by a hammer. The voice-over sounded like James Earl Jones. Their essays weren't clever. They were compelling.

Today Haig Kouyoumdjian is a psychologist. Once he was my student. In his essay on "the value of life in relation to its length" titled "The Struggle of Man and His Greatness" he wrote, "Lear does learn from his intense suffering. Though he dies the suffering made him better. The quality of goodness demands suffering to grow. This is the essence of the tragic man. When he does learn the true nature of his daughters it is too late. Too late for him. Not too late for us."

Critical thinking. Applied to the real world. Applied to themselves. It was 1994. Haig and his classmates didn't write good essays because we adapted to their learning styles. It was because they grasped the content. We didn't focus on critical thinking in isolation. We focused on thinking about something worth thinking about and made sure we built a foundation to support the analyses we undertook. It takes time. It's worth it. It's not new.

It is easy to imagine the response to the state's "modern" call for critical thinking instruction. Teachers will be hammered by demands to include it in every unit. Not everything is worthy of critical thinking. Our job as teachers is to help students be clear, systematic, and rigorous about consequential matters. There's so much inconsequential intellectual and social trivia everywhere it threatens to overwhelm everyone—and everything. Including schools.

Howard Gardner, famous for his 1983 book *Frames of Mind:*

Theory of Multiple Intelligences wrote *The Disciplined Mind: What All Students Should Understand* a decade later. In it he argued for in-depth approaches to fewer topics. His three curriculum choices: evolution, the Holocaust, and Mozart. They were his road to what he called "the understanding pathway." There are other paths. "King Lear" is one.

At the end of the unit I Xeroxed a drawing of the flawed, foolish king for each student. I attached a note:

> *Dear Scholars,*
> *The turning point of the action of King Lear is that a peasant stands up for tortured humanity. Through the tragedy itself, and through the pleasure, knowledge, and hope it brings to life, we know the freedom to be won as the domination of man by man is defeated; and in Edgar's words to Gloucester, we know the condition of that freedom: What, in ill thoughts again? Men must endure their going hence, even as their coming hither: Ripeness is all. Come on. Thank you for "coming on" through a difficult play.*
> *—Mrs. Koch*

So Alice began telling the Mock Turtle and the Gryphon her adventures from the time when she first saw the White Rabbit. She was a little nervous about it, just at first, the two creatures got so close to her, one on each side, and opened their eyes and mouths so very wide; but she gained courage as she went on.

The adventure of "King Lear" began with a trip outside the classroom. I worried about the reasons it was a bad idea—legal liability, for one. Should I get permission? A trip to a teacher's house? Then I remembered the long-ago advice I received from a wise nun—forgiveness is easier. I forged ahead.

The invitation wasn't courage on my part. It was desperation at a perennially failed unit design. It took courage for students to come.

It became an adventure for all of us. It paid off. In better discussions. Better exam scores. Better projects. The Gryphon was right.

Adventures first. Explanations after.

CHAPTER ELEVEN

Who Stole The Tarts?

*Men become civilized, not in proportion to their willingness to
believe, but in proportion to their readiness to doubt.*
—H.L. Mencken

*"Herald, read the accusation!" said the King.
On this the White Rabbit blew three blasts on the trumpet, and
then unrolled the parchment-scroll, and read as follows:—
"The Queen of Hearts, she made some tarts,
All on a summer's day:
The Knave of Hearts, he stole those tarts
And took them clean away!"
"Consider your verdict," the King said to the jury.
"Not yet, not yet!" the Rabbit hastily interrupted. "There's a great
deal to come before that!"*
—Chapter Eleven
Alice's Adventures in Wonderland

Consider the Verdict

2013. In the January cold and gloom the rumbling grew. No one admitted to the Baseball Hall of Fame—too many steroid nominees. Barry Bonds. Roger Clemens. Sammy Sosa.

No truth to the heart-rending story of Notre Dame's Heisman nominee Manti Te'o being inspired to his stellar season by the death of his girlfriend to leukemia. The girlfriend didn't exist.

Then the explosion. Lance Armstrong—seven time Tour de France winner—confessed to doping through his entire career. Headlines screamed: "Stone-Faced Armstrong Admits to Illegal Doping." "Cheater. Liar. Hero." "I'm a Flawed Character." Armstrong overcame cancer. He couldn't overcome the lure of fame and fortune; the desire to win no matter what the cost.

Cheating. I wanted a classroom climate where cheating wouldn't happen. How could I do that? I tried everything. Develop relationships. Design classes so students could control their destiny. Diminish test emphasis. It wasn't enough.

The bulky black grade book sat on the teacher's desk in the back of the room. I never used the desk. Never could figure out how anyone could sit down in a busy high school classroom. "The grade book belongs to all of us," I said. "Any time you need to check it, feel free. If you think there are mistakes, let me know." As the term unfolded, there were hundreds of "point entries" in the little squares stretching beyond each student name. Before computers they were the "record"…the only record.

The third quarter was almost over. On the way back to class after lunch one rainy afternoon a student hurried past. "Mrs. Koch, will you check on my grade today? Coach wants to know."

"Sure," I said to his retreating back.

I unlocked the door, turned on the lights and threaded through the sea of desks to the back of the classroom. The grade book wasn't there. How can that be, I thought to myself? Maybe it's under one of the enormous piles of paper? It wasn't.

I managed through the class, distracted by worry. When the final bell rang I tore the desk apart. Nothing. Searched the shelves along the back. Scanned the tables with their bulging boxes of file folders jammed below the windows. Still nothing. The grade book was my only record of student performance. Grades were due the next week. Now what? I was angry, nervous, embarrassed. I felt violated.

I hurried to the faculty room. "My grade book is gone," I said to no one in particular. Around the room people looked up. "Whoa, Kochie," said one. "Good luck with that." Sighing, I went to the dean. Explained what happened.

"You left your grade book lying round? What did you expect?"

"I expected they felt safe enough they would see it as what it was—treating them like people who do the right thing—not the stupid thing."

The dean shrugged. "I'll keep an eye out," he said. "You better check with the Studies Office about what to do. Grades are due next week."

"I KNOW that." The Director of Studies suggested a letter home, explaining what happened. A letter sent before report cards. I tossed and turned through a sleepless night. As the street light in front blinked off at dawn, I got a different idea.

I kept a detailed daily schedule on the blackboards stretching along two walls. On them I wrote what each class was doing. Sort of a "Table of Contents" for every period—and a defense against the incessant question, "What are we doing today?" I hurried to school and erased the boards. They hadn't been blank since September. It was disorienting to see the green expanse stretching like an empty lawn after the picnic is over. On one I wrote: HOW DID YOU DO THIS QUARTER? On the other: YOU TELL ME.

Students checked the boards when they came in. They were surprised.

"What's happening, Mrs. K?"

"Our grade book has disappeared," I said with a wan smile and an emphasis on "our," not "my" or even "the." "I might have lost it. Someone might have taken it." I paused. "I hope it's the first and not the second."

Students in every class squirmed as the words sunk in. Someone always said, "Wow. Cool. Then you don't know how we're doing. We all get A's." Others were angry. "I want credit for all the stuff I did. All A's isn't fair."

I listened. Then I said, "If anyone happens to find the grade book or knows where it is leave me a note. Or talk to me. After school. For now, write a letter telling me what your grade should be this quarter. Be very detailed. Think about discussions, quizzes, classwork, projects, tests." I added, "Don't forget fairy dust." They hooted. The far right column on every page was labeled "dust." Not extra credit. Sort of like decals on football helmets for extra performance. Extra courage.

Everyone got fairy dust along the way. Some when they did something. Some when they stopped doing something. We didn't talk about it much. In a room filled with stuffed dragons and Yoda squatting on the overhead, fairies weren't out of place.

"I'll use your letters as the basis for the quarter grades. Today is the one day we'll use to write these. Look at your binders to remind you what you've done. Get started."

Most teachers know how their students are doing. I knew. With few exceptions, they knew too.

Their letters were honest. "I haven't done much this term. I'm wrestling and I'm starving. I'm doing C work. I'll bring it up fourth quarter."

They were funny. "I hate saying I see myself in these books, but I do. That is really depressing. But my work is pretty good. I wish it was A but it's B. I bombed the last test. I know you remember. You called me lazy. I was."

I read their self-evaluations, agreed with most, entered grades on the Scantron sheets, and bought a new grade book.

Quarter report cards came and went. I did send a letter home… after grades were mailed. One parent complained. I set up a meeting with him, his son—and his son's bulging binder. Afterwards the father shrugged, "Looks like that grade was a gift."

"Quarter grades are progress grades," I reminded him. "He'll get there."

The next month the dean stuck his head in the classroom late one afternoon.

"I found your grade book," he laughed. "Two boys were bragging, ripping it apart and flushing it down the toilet in the 100 Building."

The two admitted they took the book. Threw it out the window. One was an underclassman I taught. Despite the theft he graduated in 1987. Eight years later a *New York Times* article caught my eye. It reported a Yale student who had been expelled several weeks before graduation for scamming his way into the Ivy League school with fake transcripts from a community college and fake recommendation letters from his old high school. The story went on to say he was caught bragging about his exploits after receiving $61,475 in student aid. My eyes widened. It was my old grade-book thief.

Many universities study cheating. Both Rutgers and Ohio State report their researchers place the number of high school students who cheat at more than 90 percent. Type A students are more likely to cheat than others, they speculate, because performance matters more. Through my career I found other instances of cheating—but not many. One, a valedictorian who was accused the day of graduation by some of his classmates of cheating on the calculus final, shrugged as he walked to the podium. "So what," he said. "I did."

When Lance Armstrong confessed he was the ringleader of an elaborate doping scheme, the interviewer asked, "Did you feel bad about it?"

"No. It was, in my view, part of the job."

The disgraced Yale student didn't feel bad either. He was defiant.

"I got Bs and Cs," he said. "What's the big deal? Some of those guys are lugheads."

"In the end," writes Hampton Stevens in the online version of *The Atlantic*, "Cheaters lose." I wonder.

The valedictorian went on to a career in investment banking. Coincidence? Unlikely. Commentary on contemporary life? Perhaps. Dangerous to a civil society? Of course.

I kept a closer eye on my grade book. I didn't leave it when I left class. I did keep it open on my desk during the day. I wasn't going to give up my idea that people behave like you expect them to. I expected them to believe in themselves. To remember other people believed in them. Christianity invites second chances. It invites forgiveness as well.

Through the years I sometimes misplaced a student paper. IF every student turned in even one page of anything every day, it amounted to 750 pieces of paper a week. If they protested they had turned something in I said, "OK, I believe you. How was it? Enter a grade in the book and circle it so I know it's what you think." They knew as well as I did how they were doing. We were in it together for the long run.

I never lost the grade book again. The year before the Yale fraud story I received a happier surprise.

The rabbit was right. There's a great deal to come before the verdict.

The first witness was the Hatter. He came in with a teacup in one hand and a piece of bread-and-butter in the other. "I beg your pardon, your Majesty," he began, "for bringing these in; but I hadn't quite finished my tea when I was sent for."
"You ought to have finished," said the King. "When did you begin?"
The Hatter looked at the March Hare, who had followed him into the court, arm in arm with the Dormouse. "Fourteenth of March, I think it was," he said.
—Chapter Eleven
Alice's Adventures in Wonderland

Not Quite Finished

*T*he course was Honors Writing. On the first day each student found a sheet of paper on their desk. In the lower left was a picture of a baby. Above it was printed:

Chances are 1 in 432 he'll be a doctor.

Chances are 1 in 350 he'll be a lawyer.

Chances are 1 in 107 he'll be a teacher.

Chances are 1 in 5 he'll be illiterate.

Along the right side I wrote in my handwriting,

Dear Students, Welcome to another chance to learn and grow. I know you have many demands on your time and often feel hassled. Remember we all care about you and would like you to have as many doors to your future open as possible. Do your best to make each day worthwhile. I'll be rooting for you. Thank you for being here. Sincerely, Mrs. Koch

I began most classes I taught, everywhere I taught, by thanking people for being there. Sometimes it didn't seem they had a choice. But there are many ways to be present and not present at the same time. That was true before technology transformed relationships. It is truer today.

The Honors course was difficult. Long papers. Lots of analysis.
Lots of reading. Lots of translating dense texts. They began with Alfred
North Whitehead's idea that language gives human beings an ability
and pleasure available to no other species. It follows, then, that we
become fully human when we use and appreciate the gift language is.
How? Through reading and writing about what we read.

The course was fun to teach. The curriculum well-suited for an
age where speed, diversity, and distraction dominate the landscape.
The class moved fast. The material was eclectic. The student profile:
juniors and seniors, our boys, plus girls from the school across the
street. Far from a distraction, girls added. Deepened discussions. Drew
different conclusions.

In 1994, I studied the new spring-term class list in dismay. Almost
all boys. Even worse—almost all seniors. I groaned. Two unwelcome
problems. Seniors begin mentally checking out the minute they step
on campus in fall. Leaving high school is a long process of disen-
gagement from a past they know to a future they don't. The present
disappears. By April they're going through the motions—barely. I
wondered. What would keep the class engaged with few girls and no
juniors? I decided dinosaurs might do it.

Michael Crichton, a Harvard-trained physician who worked his
way through school writing fiction, was a full-time novelist by 1994.
His *Jurassic Park* was a 1990 bestseller. More than a science fiction tale
about a mysterious island inhabited by dinosaurs, it raised questions
about the role of science, bioengineering, mathematical modeling.

I attached excerpts from a Crichton interview to the course syllabus with a request they buy the book. Each section of *Jurassic Park*
is an iteration on fractal analysis and chaos theory. The story wove
through the term like a beacon flashing, "This isn't tomorrow—it's
today." The novel energized the class.

The final exam had two parts:

In a detailed map explore how Jurassic Park *is a reflection of the iterations that precede each section. (60 minutes)*
Then write a 60-minute summary which compresses your map coherently and also addresses the following two observations by Michael Crichton. They are the same two observations you saw on Day One:

"I am always interested in situations where the reigning ideology does not describe the reality. To the extent that my books are entertaining, I always feel you can include a more radical underlying message. Beyond hazards of genetic engineering, Jurassic Park *also raises questions about the fundamental nature of science, and if, after 400 years, that paradigm has basically run its course.*

"I think, in a certain way, you can look at the book as being about caring for and concern for these kids. There's a sort of exposure of kids in a world created by thoughtless adults. We need to have some values, we need to impose those values upon science, not the other way around."

One student lingered after class. Thoughtful, religious, energetic, and funny, his name was Scott Drain. He was heading to Santa Clara University in the fall.

"Wow. Just wow," he said. "Dr. Koch, I REALLY need more time. I have the coolest idea. Look."

I opened the exam book. In Scott's careful handwriting he had begun:

"The use of fractals in the novel *Jurassic Park* is essential to the plot development and to uncovering the underlying message of the novel. Dr. Ian Malcolm refers to the 'fractal curve' in his explanation of why Jurassic Park will fail. His statements are the foci of the seven iterations in the novel. I have mapped out the novel in relation to a game of chess. The backdrop is a chessboard, which is essentially a fractal design."

I glanced up.

"Get it?" He was practically levitating. "The more the chess board is revealed, the closer they get to accepting the instability of the Park. I have the text to back it up."

Skimming the essay and looking at the hurriedly drawn map, I could see Scott's convincing idea. He was a good student. The course, like most of my curriculum, didn't depend on "all or none" final-exam performance.

"You've worked on this for two hours. It will be fine."

He rolled his eyes. I winked at him. Some years earlier students gave me an apron, befitting my mother-like tendency to prod them, covered with my most aggravating comments. "It's fine" was the top of the list.

"I know this is the last day of school. Let me take it home. I promise I will turn it in."

Scott's grade was assured even before the exam. I read more carefully what he had written so far. "It's a deal. When will I get the rest?"

"Soon," he said. "Gotta go. Thanks!"

It was June 3. Scott graduated. Summer came and went. The exam never appeared.

I was disappointed. The chess idea was a good one. I would have liked to see the whole analysis.

School began again. The week before Christmas I found a large brown envelope in my school mailbox. Inside was a letter, a wrinkled exam blue book, and eight stapled colored pages with increasingly cut-out centers—revealing on the last page a full chess board. The letter said,

December 14!!!!!!!
Dear Dr. Koch,
WELL, it's finally here. The test you've waited six months for. If my map looks like it's been through the war, that's because it practically has! This map has survived three trips to and from

Santa Clara, being run over by my closet door (second iteration), it's been bent, ripped, and creased, and this map has had to sit through countless times when I took it out with the intent of finishing, only to shove it back in my desk minutes later out of frustration. Here it is! Thanks for the time in the box. And thanks for the memories.
Love, Scott Drain Class of '94

Quotes framed the four sides of the completed chessboard—"Let's be clear. The planet is not in jeopardy. WE are in jeopardy." "Science can be a very deadly game indeed." "Increasingly, the mathematics will demand the courage to face its implications." "Your island is a mess. Your experiment is a mess. It has to be cleaned up."

He tweaked his essay. The new end: "We should find the courage to speak out for what is right, and not wait until it is too late."

Walking back to my cluttered crowded classroom on that cloudy winter afternoon, six months after the due date, I smiled. Sometimes it's worth waiting.

This was one of those times.

Just as this moment Alice felt a very curious sensation, which puzzled her a good deal until she made out what it was: she was beginning to grow larger again, and she thought at first she would get up and leave the court; but on second thought she decided to remain where she was as long as there was room for her.
"I wish you wouldn't squeeze so," said the Dormouse, who was sitting next to her. "I can hardly breathe."
"I can't help it," said Alice very meekly: "I'm growing."
"You've no right to grow here," said the Dormouse.
"Don't talk nonsense," said Alice more boldly: "You know you're growing too."
—Chapter Eleven
Alice's Adventures in Wonderland

A Curious Sensation

*L*apel buttons—bright bold testimony to school pride or political partisanship, or a pet point of view. "Go Spartans!" "VOTE!" I wore my collection on my jackets like a salesman's display board. They ranged from my children's Little League pictures to a turkey holding a "think ham" sign. My favorite—"What is real?"

As the AP course entered its final weeks most classes produced their own. One year on a yellow background (symbolic of Charlotte Gilman's "The Yellow Wallpaper" and her character's descent into madness) stood the center image of a terrified cartoon child, Bill Watterson's Calvin. Around him were phrases alluding to the long journey we had taken together. There were two versions: "If grades aren't real what am I doing building a 3-D essay in the dark on the river?"—The other offered: "In the flicker... Do I dare? A 3-D hanging what?" Some years there were unicorns. Or simply "We survived."

Advanced Placement is like a cross-country squad—individuals who work against themselves and for the group; push boundaries, focus on distant hills; or a baseball team—using their unique position skills to make something better than they were as individual contributors. They weren't simply students studying stories. They were the story.

The final exam was titled "Last at Bat." One hour. Time mattered. For them. For me. Left to their own devices they could write for days. The prompt:

Write the story of your life in AP English. You are as much of a character as the characters we met. Include as many specific comments about the books as you can. Begin like this…Once upon a time there was a young man/woman who awoke one day and found himself trapped in a box.

The essays were long, detailed, by turns funny and heart-rending. Their endings were poignant, proud, passionate…

Problems aside we finished, doing a great job. And "at last the moment had come…" (from Crime and Punishment*) for the best work of my young career. Although my thesis is not yet completed I feel confident it's better than good. When I look at AP graduation I feel a certain renewal. Again from C and P, '… that is the beginning of a new story—the story of the gradual renewal of a man, the story of his gradual regeneration, of his passing from one world into another, of his initiation into a new unknown life. That might be the subject of a new story but our present story is ended.' —Dan*

Our hero looks upon his future with optimism and free of worry. He has escaped the darkness of the box and is ready for his next challenge. He is ready to face the boxes of college and then those of life. It will be a hard battle, but one he knows he can win. He's already started. —Tony

As the young man sat pondering his thoughts, he came to a conclusion. IF he were to choose any single method of escaping the box—tragic, heroic, alienated, super—he would fail because he wouldn't be complete. Only a combination can propel him. All the characters he met can help him. Is the box getting smaller, or did I just grow bigger?—Michael

Teaching is like parenting…long lonely periods of exhaustion punctuated by exuberant moments of joy. One year two of us hatched a scheme to teach the AP class together. We came from different backgrounds. We had different educations. We were a teaching version of "The Odd Couple." My friend was compulsively organized. Linear. Hundreds of papers didn't faze him. I was forever fumbling for lost overhead transparencies. Misplaced visual aids. Special bell schedules he knew by heart. I didn't like outlines. Mostly because they look organized but they usually didn't have any internal logic. I liked to draw diagrams of student ideas. I told myself it was good for students to see different styles in action. In reality it drove them crazy. Us too. We adapted. So did they.

That year one student began his final: "Once upon a time there was a young man who awoke one day and found himself trapped in a box. A very colorful box. A short psychotic lady, with a neurotic short sidekick of a man, set out to prove that grades aren't real—only learning is real."

Rudy Schulze was the "sidekick." A piano player, gourmet cook, talented speaker, and classically trained former Jesuit, he was the Director of Admissions and one of my favorite colleagues. Schools don't let two teachers fill one position in a way that both are in the classroom simultaneously. It is too expensive. We managed, through a combination of Rudy sneaking out of his office every day for two hours, teaching without being paid extra, and the quiet willingness of the Christian Brothers to look the other way. When he died of a heart attack several years later, our one year together became even more special. Not for the teaching. For the friendship. Rudy was 50 years old when he died. We thought we'd have more time.

Students enrolled in AP for all kinds of reasons. Reading their final exams reminded me. Some entered indifferent. Some through scheduling snafus. Some wanted advanced courses on their transcripts. None were looking for more friends. Yet the relationships they built through months of working together mattered at least as much as what they learned from the books.

Tim was an example. Prickly, self-absorbed, independent, theatrical, he wasn't happy adjusting his busy schedule to work with others, or with the comments I had been scrawling across his papers for months: "Ask more questions. Are you thinking? Where's the support? The logic in this paper leads nowhere." Gradually his work improved. So did his disposition.

The last week of class one of his partners lost her grandfather. Tim concluded his essay: "The young man did something he had never done. He put aside work on his thesis and called in sick to rehearsal to spend the afternoon and evening with his grieving friend. This was the greatest lesson the young man learned in the box. He learned the value of true friends. He could not allow them to experience loneliness and alienation the way the characters in the class's books do. The young man learned that learning meant a lot, but that people matter more."

Growing. Tim was a big person with a small heart. His outside appearance didn't change in one school year. Inside was a different story. It takes a long time to learn what things are real. Compassion is one of those things.

When aggressive academically driven competitive students figure that out—it's a victory. Rudy was ecstatic. So was I.

Alice decided to remain at court as long as there was room for her. Then it was time to leave.

Rudy and I smiled at each other as we finished Tim's exam. Our work was finished.

Time for us to leave too.

Part Six

Celebrate

Laughter and Tears

A harmless hilarity and a buoyant cheerfulness are not infrequent concomitants of genius; and we are never more deceived THAN WHEN we mistake gravity for greatness, solemnity for science, and pomposity for erudition.
—Charles Caleb Colton

CHAPTER TWELVE

ALICE'S EVIDENCE

*All men should strive to learn before they die, what they are run-
ning from, and to, and why.*
—James Thurber

*Alice jumped up in such a hurry that she tipped over the jury-
box with the edge of her skirt, upsetting all the jury-men on to
the heads of the crowd below, and there they lay sprawling about,
reminding her very much of a globe of gold-fish she had acciden-
tally upset the week before.*
*"The trial cannot proceed," said the King, in a very grave voice,
"until all the jurymen are back in their proper places—all," he
repeated with great emphasis, looking hard at Alice as he said so.
Alice looked at the jury-box, and saw that, in her haste, she had
put the Lizard in head downwards, and the poor little thing was
waving its tail about in a melancholy way, being quite unable to
move. She got it out again, and put it right; "not that it signifies
much," she said to herself; "I should think it would be quite as
much use in the trial one way up as the other."*
—Chapter Twelve
Alice's Adventures in Wonderland

PROPER PLACES

Four women gathered around the conference table. All were
graduate students at Chapman University College. All

administrators. All with master's degrees. One had a Ph.D. They were there to comply with California's arcane licensing requirements for public education. Once a week they made their way from far-flung northern California cities for the required Moral and Ethical Leadership course.

Between class meetings I visited their campuses…the California State Prison in Vacaville, two Napa middle schools once designated "Distinguished"—now called "underperforming" as enrollments became overwhelmingly Spanish speaking—and a Vallejo special education director whose budgets were shrinking as demand for service grew. I wondered. What could I offer them?

After a week of driving hundreds of miles among their campuses it struck me. The state and the university used a "one size fits all" set of standards for wildly different circumstances and for professionals who had years of education and experience already.

The course reading was chosen by a "custodian" from the main campus in southern California. The choices were earnest, wonky, and detached—case studies of moral decision making, philosophies of power, academic journal articles with titles like: "The Practical Value of Philosophical Thought for the Ethical Dimension of Educational Leadership."

We were in northern California. The students arrived exhausted, preoccupied, resigned to checking off the course for their license renewals. I had my directions. We were all in our proper places. Easy to monitor. Enervating to implement.

I remembered a conversation with my first principal.

"Should I learn the Catholic catechism since I'm teaching in a Catholic school?" I asked in a burst of enthusiasm for my new job.

"No need to learn the long form," the elderly nun said. "The short form is perfect."

"What is the short form?"

"There are different versions. I like this one: 'What is the chief end of man? To love God, and serve one another.'"

Her cherubic face crinkled in a smile. "That's all you need. That's all any of us need."

I didn't believe that was ALL we need, but it goes a long way. I asked the graduate students what they needed to make the term more useful for them.

"Let's use our own campus issues for case studies."

"Let's read some women theorists too."

"Let's talk about consistency in ethics."

"Let's eat dinner while we work."

I had one addition myself. "Let's read Howard Gardner's *Good Work: When Excellence and Ethics Meet*. It's dedicated to John Gardner, former President of the Carnegie Foundation for the Advancement of Teaching and winner of the Presidential Medal of Freedom. We'll talk about it at our last meeting…a dinner at my house. My gift to you."

It's been seven years since Bill Gates left his day job at Microsoft to concentrate on the Bill and Melinda Gates Foundation. His enterprise is booming. With Warren Buffet as a trustee, the foundation plans to spend three billion dollars in the next few years on education. They have concluded that increasing achievement is as simple as removing bad teachers, identifying good ones, and paying them more. On this theory they are investing in Tampa, Memphis, Pittsburg, and a charter consortium in Los Angeles. It will favor or penalize teachers based on test performance.

Teachers are critical to good schools. But teachers and their administrators are holding mirrors up to the communities they serve. Without the candor and willingness to look at all the players in a social system, no amount of money will make a lasting difference.

My graduate students didn't need more money. They needed more time to reflect. They needed more honest dialogue about systemic changes transforming the country. They needed more people celebrating their successes. Cheering their courage. I reshaped the curriculum around their needs, their circumstances, the challenges their own teachers and students faced every day—drugs, poverty, reading levels hovering around sixth grade for the prisoners, even lower for second-language and special-needs students. Broken lives.

We spent time reading Harvard professor Carol Gilligan. In 1970 she became a research assistant for Lawrence Kohlberg, famous for his stage theory of moral development. She went on to study girls and to criticize Kohlberg for his concentration on only men and boys. Worse, from her view, the male view of individual rights and rules was placed higher than the female view of caring as a higher quality. The quality of care came to dominate the course.

At the final dinner celebration I gave them each a children's board book. On the front a young boy has his hand outstretched toward the moon. The title—*Twinkle, Twinkle, Little Star*. On the back—"How I wonder what you are?" It echoed John Gardner, the wise, caring scholar, community builder, and former Secretary of HEW, who wrote about himself, "Looking back over the years I see a California boy finding his way through life, endlessly challenged, surmounting obstacles, falling on his face, regretting that he hadn't done better, always studying, always trying, always wondering."

Alice knew having the jury in their proper places was no guarantee of a fair trial. I knew the course material was no guarantee that any of the problems my students faced would be solved. But I knew the caring, the chance to wonder together, mattered. To them. To me. Gardner was right. I wrote his message on their place cards.

"The first and last task of a leader is to keep hope alive."

We did that for one another.

"If there's no meaning in it," said the King, "that saves a world of trouble, you know, as we needn't try to find any. And yet I don't know," he went on, spreading out the verses on his knee, and looking at them with one eye; "I seem to see some meaning in them after all."
—Chapter Twelve
Alice's Adventures in Wonderland

MEANING AFTER ALL

Celebrations. Fewer are bigger than Olympic openings. In 2012 Oscar-winning director Danny Boyle orchestrated the London summer games opening ceremony in an hours-long tribute to British history and culture. Headlines proclaimed "Queen, Corgis, and James Bond Open the Games." There was famous British music. In one sequence a stunt double for the Queen and Agent 007 parachuted into the stadium. In another some of the well-known villains of children's books appeared as oversized puppets, including Captain Hook, Cruella de Vil, and Voldemort.

"It was a celebration for its own sake," said Boyle. "But it makes a more serious point about the importance of literature and literacy. If you can read and write you're free or can fight for your freedom. That's worth celebrating any time."

Every year I bought a large blue spiral planner to sketch out weekly lessons. Even though the lessons never went quite as expected, we all knew the general direction we were heading. At the top of the cover page was one telephone number, transferred from year to year, next to a name: Evelyn.

Evelyn lived near the high school in a quiet residential neighborhood. She ran a home cake-decorating business. Her concoctions were delicious and fresh. I began buying large sheet cakes for my sophomore classes at the end of the year. I wanted to celebrate them. Their risk-taking. Their effort. Their energy. I would arrive with the huge cakes topped with the green and white school colors. "Congratulations! WE did it!" danced across the icing. We'd debrief, turn in binders, tease one another. Sometimes there were gifts for me, pulled out of paper bags or backpacks. One year I got Mickey Mouse ears. I wore them for a decade. I had gifts for them too—calendars for the disorganized, Lysol for some gym bags, promises for a lifetime supply of pencils for students who never had one.

The AP class held a "graduation breakfast" at the nearby public golf club. Its restaurant was at the end of a windy drive on a hill overlooking the city. Students arrived carrying their bound "senior theses"—what I called their "tribute to twelve years of school and the people who taught me along the way." I invited school administrators, the department chair, sometimes college professors or colleagues from other schools. Students stood, read their title aloud, and presented the papers to a school representative who shook their hand and thanked them. There were certificates for everything—most sleep-deprived, worst sense of humor, person who passed while doing the least reading—all accompanied by laughter and tears as the community we had been slipped away into a different present.

Years later a university student I was teaching lingered after class one evening.

"I am doing my first Back to School night tomorrow," she said. "Can I run my presentation by you?"

"Go for it."

The young woman taught second grade in a wealthy suburb. She was organized, detailed, armed with a dozen handouts to show how activities aligned with the standards. She had weekly goals, unit goals, semester goals, year-end outcomes.

"Looks very complete," I said, cringing a little. "Are you sure you need to share so much detail?"

"I want them to have confidence in me," she said. I wondered if it might be overkill. It felt like technical specifications for a computer program more than general operating instructions for a classroom.

"Good luck tomorrow. Let us know how it goes."

The following week she returned, dropped into her seat, and rested her head on her briefcase.

"So…how did your Back to School night turn out?" I asked, though it was obvious the answer was not going to be what I wanted to hear—or, more important, what she wanted to hear.

"I explained EVERYTHING we do," she fretted. "They took it for granted. They don't understand how hard it is to cover it all. And then one man asked a question. Other people were nodding. They had the same thought."

"What did he ask?"

"He raised his hand and said, 'We expect you to do your job and it looks like you're doing it. But when do they get to have fun? They're seven years old.'"

"What did you say?"

"We don't have time for fun."

A single tear slipped from the corner of her eye.

As the Wonderland trial begins, the King asks Alice what she knows. She responds, "Nothing."

> *"That's very important," the King said, turning to the jury. They were just beginning to write this down on their slates, when the White Rabbit interrupted: "Unimportant, your Majesty means, of course," he said, in a very respectful tone, but frowning and making faces at him as he spoke.*
>
> *"Unimportant, of course, I meant," the King hastily said, and went on to himself in an undertone, "important—unimport-*

ant—unimportant—important—" as if he were trying which word sounded best.

Some of the jury wrote it down "important," and some "unimportant." Alice could see this, as she was near enough to look over their slates; "but it doesn't matter a bit," she thought to herself.

The young teacher's presentation had all the important elements. All but one—space for diversions. It seems unimportant. Irresponsible. In the end, though, the celebrations—planned or spontaneous—are the iridescent colors that light up school days. Learning the craft of teaching took me a decade. Mastering the art of teaching was never finished.

In the end, my individual memories of lesson plans and curriculum design expanded into collages of overlapping images: students laughing, lounging in the classroom at lunch and after school, hanging holiday decorations from the acoustic ceiling panels, draping Christmas lights around plastic trees, lugging milk crates across campus for parties, taking pictures (before cell phones) during student presentations, singing "happy un-birthday to you" for summer celebrants. All of us cheering classmates who passed their driver's test, made a team, snagged a prom date, went a year without a speeding ticket, got a part in a drama production.

Part of the curriculum? No.

Trivial? No.

Meaningless? No.

They were ways to celebrate. Ways to remember there is a magical child inside everyone. Whether students are 4, 14, or 40—fun tempers the stress and worry that nibbles at the corners of every life.

Students work hard. Harder outside class than in. Sometimes it is impossible to tell what is important and what is not in the present moment. What is clear is that students and adults see the world through different lenses. They spend hours in worlds we never visit.

We can't. We belong to yesterday. They belong to tomorrow.

The King was right. There was meaning in the verses the White Rabbit read at the trial. It just takes time to figure out. Time the Queen didn't allow in Wonderland. Time teachers can't snatch from the avalanche of expectations they face in a shrinking world.

The longer I taught, the less I wrote in my blue planner. But Evelyn the cake lady was never eliminated. Young people inherit a world they didn't create. Thanking them and celebrating them for staying in the game was important.

And it was fun.

"Oh, I've had such a curious dream!" said Alice. And she told her sister, as well as she could remember them, all these strange Adventures of hers that you have just been reading about; and, when she had finished, her sister kissed her, and said "It was a curious dream, dear, certainly; but now run in to your tea: it's getting late." So Alice got up and ran off, thinking while she ran, as well she might, what a wonderful dream it had been.
—Chapter Twelve
Alice's Adventures in Wonderland

A WONDERFUL DREAM

T he Heisenberg Uncertainty Principle says physics is bound with probabilities. The bedrock of quantum theory, it implies that even if one has all the information there is to be had about a system, its future behavior cannot be determined exactly. Even if I had known everything about Catholic schools I couldn't have predicted what happened to me. In a graduation speech one year I explained. Gazing over the thousand people gathered in the warm sun, my eyes scanned the crowd. People proud. People sad. People relieved. No one gets through school alone. I was looking at the rest of the story. The graduates sat on risers behind the speaker's podium. Midway through my speech I shifted the microphone and turned sideways to speak directly to the rows and rows of emerald green caps and gowns.

"A friend told me schools are just schools—people are just people—and I would find the same apathy and impersonal system here that I saw in many other places. But that has not been the case.

You've been friendly—whether you knew me or not you always had time to say hello.

You've been fun to be around. All of us have made demands on you—teachers, coaches, parents, bosses, girlfriends—and despite us you kept your sense of humor in tact.

You've been honest about your likes and dislikes about everything—from the books we read (which you thought were lame) to the clothes I wore (which you also thought were lame).

You've been critical when you didn't think I was being relevant or when you thought I was going off the deep end. We've had wonderful arguments about what is the deep end.

You understood, as the President of Brown University said last month—one way to paralyze people is to overwhelm them with trivia—and you tried not to let that happen to you.

You've been patient with the weirdness that is part of all schools.

Most important, you've asked questions every day—questions about your faith, about your friends, about your world. Most of the interesting questions don't have answers but they're still worth asking.

There's a light in your eyes. Sometimes I've seen it shining clear and steady. Sometimes I've seen it flickering through your tears and hurt.

So it turns out my friend was wrong. This is not just another school and you are not ordinary people. But I was wrong too. I thought I was going to be teaching you and I ended up loving you. This was a pretty annoying complication—something not covered in UCLA's teacher training. It made the stakes much higher every day. So I haven't really been a teacher here but a learner with you, trying to figure out ways to encourage you and to challenge you not to take the easy roads.

There is no question the easy roads go somewhere—but where they go is never as satisfying as a journey made with more vision and more commitment. It's like the Confucian saying, 'Those who seek only the small advantages never achieve great things.' I wanted you to realize you can be key players in the information society—but it is a society where the passport to personal dignity and economic security is a first rate education.

As I look at you I am reminded of Virgil's *Aeneid*. In it the Trojan and son of Venus becomes the founder of Rome. As Troy is conquered and ransacked by the Greeks, Aeneas leads an army of survivors to escape by sea. In doing so he lifts his aging father to his back and grasps the hand of his little son who runs by his side. In his father he is carrying, protecting, and preserving the past; in his son he is taking care of those who will live in the future. My hope for you is you will keep the best of your past while creating a better future in the borderless world on the horizon.

My favorite Shel Silverstein poem is called 'The Bridge.' It says,

This bridge will only take you halfway there
To those mysterious lands you long to see.
Through gypsy camps and swirling Arab fairs
And moonlit woods where unicorns run free.
So come and walk awhile with me
And share the twisting trails and wondrous worlds I've known.
But this bridge will only take you halfway there
The last few steps you'll have to take alone.

I'll look for you on the other side of the bridge. You'll look different—still handsome, maybe rounder, a few wrinkles, less hair—but I'll recognize you. It's the light in your eyes that will give you away. It's the light that will always make the shadows of hopelessness and ignorance disappear. It's the light of love. Keep it shining all the days of your life."

Alice's sister tells her it's late and time to go.

But her sister sat still just as she left her, leaning her head on her hand, watching the setting sun, and thinking…how this same little sister of hers would, in the after-time, be herself a grown woman…and how she would gather about her other children, and make their eyes bright and eager with many a strange tale, perhaps even the dream of Wonderland of long ago.

Alice and I both found what we were looking for. A place where people grow. Where they find the courage to change and heart to help. Where surprises are routine. Where White Rabbits are normal. Where lessons come from unexpected sources.

Where there are always more questions than answers.

Wonderland.

"Hold your tongue!" said the Queen, turning purple.
"I won't!" said Alice.
"Off with her head!" the Queen shouted at the top of her voice.
Nobody moved.
"Who cares for you?" said Alice (she had grown to her full size by this time). "You're nothing but a pack of cards!"
At this the whole pack rose up into the air, and came flying down upon her; she gave a little scream, half of fright and half of anger, and tried to beat them off, and found herself lying on the bank, with her head in the lap of her sister, who was gently brushing away some dead leaves that had fluttered down from the trees upon her face.
"Wake up, Alice dear!" said her sister. "Why, what a long sleep you've had!"
—Chapter Twelve
Alice's Adventures in Wonderland

EPILOGUE

We expect schools and societies to reflect each other. Not just in terms of subjects taught, but also with respect to how they are organized and function. Three heuristics compete. For some, schools exist to socialize students to adapt to the world's economic, political, and social institutions. Socialization means molding individuals to fit existing cultural practices and requirements. Today that looks like specialized "academies" within large public institutions.

A second view is schools as places used by those in power to maintain dominance in the social order. As sites which preserve inequality. People react by forming their own independent schools, charter schools, home schools. Many drop out.

A third position sees schools as made up of actors who interpret meanings, rules, and norms to make social interaction possible. As places where people learn to understand why things work the way they do. Often in wealthier communities or cities compulsive about correctness, these schools look inclusive. Often they simply lack focus. Something for everyone easily becomes nothing for anyone.

Catholic schools don't fit neatly into any single model. They are as varied as the church itself and the religious orders that run them. Some are harsh, almost Dickens-like. Some are country clubs for the cloistered. Some are storefronts. Some are parochial in the worst sense. But some are compassionate, caring places with wide arms and a steady focus on a few fundamental values—chief among them to love one another. They are places that believe mistakes are part of growing, but where consequences exist. Where neither anarchy nor apathy find a home.

Teachers occupy a peculiar spot in our culture. We say we value them. We say they are professionals. Yet they are often treated as parts of a larger machine...a machine over which they have little control. As public schools are ravaged by competing self-interests and a disintegrating social fabric, Catholic schools offer special gifts. In many I found a philosophy grounded in the idea that human beings are reflections of something eternal. Something essential. If people don't reach their potential, if they skate through life like Fiyero, the feckless prince in "Wicked," we all lose. They are champions for a civil, caring society.

For years I walked around mumbling, "Martin Luther was right," as the institutional church careened from one catastrophe to another. He might have been right about the church. He wasn't talking about its schools.

In frustration Alice tossed the incompetent playing cards in the air at the knave's trial. She had grown up. She had the courage to do what she thought herself, not what the system demanded. At the outset of my career, the UCLA "Teaching Tips" weren't useful either.

I threw them out. Over a very long time I grew as well. Along the way I made my own list:

- Believe school matters. Every day.
- Create community. Be part of it.
- Find mentors.
- Take chances. Give chances.
- Start where students are. Not where the curriculum is.
- Tell them where they're going. Why it matters.
- Ask a few important questions. Align the instruction.
- Challenge them. Coach them. Celebrate them.
- Give choices when you can. Reasons when you can't.
- Care about them.
- Thank them.
- Thank them again.

In 1612 Galileo saw the planet Neptune and thought it was a star. It wasn't discovered officially until 1846. I thought teaching was a vocation I could master. Thirty years later I realized I would always be an apprentice. Tomorrow has new mysteries. They'll need new solutions. I wonder what we'll see.

In wonder all philosophy began,
In wonder it ends.
—Samuel Taylor Coleridge

ACKNOWLEDGMENTS

A person's life in education begins with teachers who inspired them. In my case the list would be longer than any book. Among those to whom I am indebted: Edna Bruce, my dynamic high school Civics instructor who believed excellence was within everyone's reach; Mildred Robeck at the University of Oregon and Candy Boyd at Saint Mary's College, for teaching me about reading; Alan Cohen and Joan Hyman at the University of San Francisco, for challenging me to design better lessons; Sister Jean Heinisch, Jack O'Leary, and Sister Veronica Skillin, mentors who coached me about campus life in different schools; Rudy Schulze and Nancy Jokerst, who showed me the power of faith in action; Joan Thisius and Carolyn Kelso at Chapman University College for expanding my opportunities to serve a wider community; Kathy Gannon Briggs, Brother Tom Westberg, Barbara Sullivan, Jan Tupaj-Farthing, and Joan Kreamer, whose administrative skills made life better for so many.

Thanks to the Sisters of the Holy Names of Jesus and Mary, the Sisters of Notre Dame de Namur, and especially to the Brothers of the Christian Schools for giving me a chance to work in such remarkable schools. To the Society of Jesus for the scholarship opportunity to study at USF later in my career.

To my parents, who never made me turn off the light at midnight when I was still reading. To my husband who navigated decades of paper piles, stacked books, and teenagers that weren't ours wandering through the house. To my own children, Geoff and Brad, for reminding me how to play.

To Juliana Kleist-Corwin for her writing advice and the Monday writers group for their support. To Patricia Marshall, talented editor and designer who brings books to life.

To my colleagues everywhere, men and women dedicated to the

service of others, often in extraordinarily difficult circumstances.

In the sixteenth century Montaigne observed, "The great secret of life is to learn lessons, not to teach them." To my students, who taught me lessons every day, and to their parents, who shared their remarkable young people. It was an honor.

Thank you all.

Anne Koch

Pleasanton, California

2013

ABOUT THE AUTHOR

*A*nne Koch spent more than three decades working with students from preschool to graduate school. A UCLA graduate, she has a lifetime credential in English, is a licensed Reading Specialist, and holds advanced degrees from Saint Mary's College of California and the University of San Francisco. She is the recipient of many awards for her scholarship and teaching, including the Saint Mary's College Reading Leadership Award, the USF outstanding doctoral dissertation award for her work on improving reading comprehension across disciplines, and the LaSallian Educator of the Year award from the Brothers of the Christian Schools. She was honored by Chapman University College as its Teacher of the Year in 2004 and has received Outstanding Teacher awards from the University of California at San Diego, at Santa Barbara, and Brown University for her work in preparing students for college study.

She is the author of a three-volume memoir focused on growing up in a Navy family in a time of dramatic social change for women titled *River Journeys*. The Alice in Wonderland memoir is the third book in a collection of book-length essays that also includes *It's All About the Story—Composing a Life in Books* and *Finding Home—A Memoir of Arts and Crafts*.

A retired teacher, professor, and high school administrator, she is the mother of two grown children and five grandchildren. She lives in Pleasanton, California, with her husband and Welsh corgi, where she is an enthusiastic porcelain painter and writer working on the fourth book in her essay series, *Flashing Yellow—At the Intersection of Yesterday and Tomorrow*.

CPSIA information can be obtained at www.ICGtesting.com
Printed in the USA
LVOW12s0813220713

343894LV00003B/6/P